THE CALGARY FLAMES

The Hottest Players & Greatest Games

Peter Boer

OVER TIME BOOKS

© 2007 by OverTime Books
First printed in 2007   10 9 8 7 6 5 4 3 2 1
Printed in Canada

The Publisher: OverTime Books is an imprint of Éditions de la Montagne Verte

Library and Archives Canada Cataloguing in Publication

Boer, Peter, 1977–
    The Calgary Flames / Peter Boer

    Includes bibliographical references.
    ISBN 13: 978-1-897277-07-2
    ISBN 10: 1-897277-07-5

    1. Calgary Flames (Hockey team)—History. I. Title.

GV848.C28B62 2007   796.962'6409712338   C2007-900296-X

Project Director: J. Alexander Poulton
Project Editor: Brian Crane
Cover Image: Courtesy of Getty Images Sport; photo by Jeff Vinnick/Stringer

PC: P5

Contents

Dedication

To Dan, Aly and Jamie
For making every hockey game a great memory.

Acknowledgements

My heartfelt gratitude, as everything else in life, goes first and foremost to my mother. To Jay Poulton, who keeps returning the favor, even though he doesn't have to—you are a true friend. To Brian, for what was a seamless, painless edit on such short notice. To Dad, for loving the Flames when no one else did. And lastly, my thanks to Opa and Uncle Dave, for indulging my interests whenever I came to visit.

One Night in Montréal

A s the clock counted down in hockey's most hallowed shrine, all eyes focused on "The Mustache."

For the first time in history, another team was going to beat the Montréal Canadiens on their home ice to win the Stanley Cup. Despite more than 70 years of hockey history, no team besides *Les Glorieux* had ever carried hockey's holy grail around the expanse of the Montréal Forum. But on that May night in 1989, the Flames, a team from Atlanta now playing out of Calgary, would win their first Stanley Cup in franchise history.

Within the team's ranks, there were a handful of first-time Cup winners. Doug Gilmour, the enduring center who had left St. Louis under a cloud of suspicion. Jim Peplinski, the hard-nosed, 29-year-old Flames "lifer" who never gave less than everything he had. Mike Vernon, the sometimes cocky but always focused goaltender who was born and raised in Calgary. Joe Nieuwendyk, holder of the rookie scoring record for the team. Theoren Fleury, a sparkplug 20-year-old with a feisty attitude that belied his small stature. Al MacInnis, who wielded the hardest slapshot in hockey. Gary Suter. Rick Wamsley. Joey Mullen. Tim Hunter. None of them had ever won hockey's ultimate prize.

Then there was Lanny McDonald, the man who had come to symbolize everything great about the Calgary Flames. McDonald had scored 60 goals fresh off his trade to the Flames from the Toronto Maple Leafs and only months before the Stanley Cup win had notched his 500th career goal. The man with the giant red mustache had proven himself to be Calgary's most potent leader and recognizable face. Now, in what would be his last game in his last season in the NHL, Lanny McDonald had become a Stanley Cup champion.

That he would win the most coveted prize in all of hockey on the ice of the Montréal Forum was more historically significant than many knew. McDonald had scored his very first goal as a Toronto Maple Leaf against the vaunted Habs on their home ice. Now, 16 years later, playing for a different team, McDonald scored the last goal of his career on that same sheet of ice. As the puck crossed the line, McDonald's arms shot into the air, holding his stick aloft as he rounded the ice to celebrate with his teammates. With McDonald's goal on the board, the Cup was as good as theirs.

The fans of *Les Glorieux* applauded and cheered politely, even though their team had come up short in the six-game series. By the time the Cup made its way on to the ice, even those Flames players who had not dressed for the game and wore only their red long johns were running around, hugging their sweaty teammates in celebration. What happened next was predictable and timeless. One by one, the Flames rounded the ice at the Forum, hoisting the Cup aloft, kissing it and passing it from player to player. Once the rounds were completed, the Flames crowded around the Stanley Cup for a team photo, a tradition started by the Edmonton Oilers not many years before.

During the 1989 regular season, the Flames had torn their way to a first-place finish in the NHL through a combination of skill, talent and sheer physical strength. Being in first place is typically a harbinger of doom to an NHL team, but the Flames relished their "best of" status. In the playoffs, they dispatched the Vancouver Canucks, the Los Angeles Kings, and the Chicago Blackhawks and then faced off against the number two team from the regular season, the Montréal Canadiens.

The Canadiens, who had carved out their niche during the season as a team with a suffocating defense, boasted no small share of talent. Brian Skrudland, Guy Carbonneau, Craig Ludwig, Bobby Smith, Chris Chelios and Bob Gainey formed the core of the team, and Patrick Roy minded the pipes. Many of these players had been members of the Canadiens' 1986 Dream Team. Roy had been its hero. That team had dealt the Flames a stinging five-game defeat in the Cup final. Now, in the 1989 Stanley Cup showdown, the best faced off against the best.

But history didn't repeat itself. Despite their legacy and their talent, the Habs could not find a way to beat the Flames, and Calgary stood, for the first time ever, atop the rest of the NHL. They had been dispatched from the playoffs 14 times before in Atlanta and Calgary. But now, they looked down on the rest of the league as champions.

Unfortunately, an exodus started that off-season. Lanny McDonald, as predicted, retired. Surprisingly, Jim Peplinski also bowed out of professional hockey, choosing to sell cars instead. In a move dubbed "the worst trade in hockey," Doug Gilmour was traded away from the team. Within the next four years, Joey Mullen,

Al MacInnis, Mike Vernon and Gary Suter were all traded or left the team. In 1997, the Flames missed the playoffs for the first time since moving to Calgary.

Seven seasons of disappointment, misery and outright dejection followed as the Flames plumbed new lows in the cellar of the NHL. It seemed all they could do was lose.

The fans who had watched in 1989 and who had celebrated wildly when their Flames had finally achieved playoff glory, were now watching them struggle to make the playoffs. They remembered the excitement of 1989 and wondered if anything like it would ever happen again.

Chapter One

Ice in Atlanta

Ice hockey and Atlanta, Georgia. On its face, the pairing seems one of polar opposites.

In this muggy southern state, the temperature rarely dips below the freezing point in winter but soars as high as 100 degrees in the summer. Very little about it conjures up images of hockey. There are no vast sheets of open ice, no piles of snow and seldom, if ever, a need for a toque.

But the people of Atlanta know their sports. The Atlanta Braves have been a fixture in Major League Baseball since 1966. The Atlanta Falcons of the National Football League set up tent that same year. The Atlanta Hawks of the National Basketball Association moved to Georgia from St. Louis after the 1967–68 season.

Within that one three-year period, a team from each of America's three most popular sports hung a shingle in Atlanta. The city suddenly overflowed with sports riches.

At the same time, hockey was trying to make inroads into the sports market of the United States. Hockey had been a fixture south of the border since the inception of the National Hockey League (NHL). But the four American teams that formed the "Original Six" of the league— the Boston Bruins, the Chicago Blackhawks, the Detroit Red Wings and the New York Rangers— played only in the northern reaches of the country where snow fell and lakes froze over in winter. The start of the 1967–68 season heralded a permanent change in the NHL as teams began to play in Pittsburgh, Los Angeles, St. Louis, Philadelphia, Minnesota and California, doubling the size of the league overnight. The NHL also faced a threat in the form of the upstart World Hockey Association (WHA), a professional league that was using big contracts and relaxed age restrictions to siphon off much of the young talent pool. WHA franchises were springing up across the continent, and there were two markets in particular that the NHL was concerned about: New York and Atlanta. New York, home already to the NHL's New York Rangers, was still big enough to host another professional hockey team, and Atlanta, having just completed construction of a 15,000-seat arena for the NBA's Atlanta Hawks, seemed ripe for the picking.

In Atlanta, Tom Cousins and a group of Georgia businessmen were intent on introducing hockey as the fourth professional sport to a region that, seven years before, had been without any. Together they backed Atlanta's bid to win a new NHL franchise. Eager to cut the WHA's growth off at the knees, the NHL needed little convincing. Although there had been no plans to expand the league for the 1972–73 season, new franchises were approved in both Long Island and Atlanta. Atlanta's new team would make their home in the recently finished 15,000-seat Omni Coliseum, but they still needed a name.

Cousins and his partners sought inspiration in the South's turbulent history. Georgia had been a part of the Confederacy during the U.S. Civil War from 1861 to 1865 and had suffered heavy losses when the Union army, under the command of General William T. Sherman, fought its way through the state. The Confederates fortified themselves at Atlanta trying to stop his charge, but Sherman surrounded the city, forcing them to retreat. To solidify his victory, Sherman burned their military installations and much of the city to the ground.

In honor of the state's history, Cousins and his business partners named their new team the Atlanta Flames and chose a letter "A" set ablaze from within as the insignia. With a place to play and a name the public could easily identify with, it was now time to start building a team.

The Flames ownership intended to make the team as competitive as possible, despite their expansion franchise label. So President William Putnam set his sights on Cliff Fletcher, a man who could spot talent and had a knack for motivating players.

Fletcher had been doing quite well for himself in the NHL. He had served as a scout with the Montréal Canadiens, hockey's most prestigious team, for 10 years before being hired by the 1967 expansion team St. Louis Blues. Within two years, he was named assistant general manager. Over the next four years of his tenure, the Blues appeared in the Stanley Cup finals three times. That the team never won a game in the finals was a matter overlooked by many. On January 12, 1972, Putnam, who had been appointed president of the team only three weeks earlier, named Fletcher general manager of the Atlanta Flames.

Fletcher knew from the outset that selling hockey in the Atlanta market would be a challenge. But he also believed Atlanta's sports fans would be eager to embrace something new.

"Atlanta, in a lot of respects, had a satisfactory amount of hockey interest," said Fletcher. "The people who went to the games were wildly enthusiastic and supportive."

Fletcher's first move as general manager was to search for a talented coach who could inspire players and draw in fans who might not be familiar with the sport of hockey. Fletcher decided to mix hockey greatness with leadership, anointing former Montréal Canadiens forward Bernard "Boom Boom" Geoffrion as Atlanta's head coach. In 883 games—all but 117 of which had been spent with the Canadiens—Geoffrion had recorded 393 goals and 429 assists. His nickname stemmed from the booming slapshot he used to assail NHL goalies, a shot he claimed to have "invented" as a young boy.

After retiring from play in 1968, Geoffrion had briefly coached the New York Rangers. Now under Fletcher's tenure, Geoffrion was given a chance few of his coaching colleagues had ever experienced. He would be the first coach of a new team in its first season in the NHL. That team was like a blank slate, and he was free to inscribe his own strategy into it.

The team that took to the ice for the beginning of the 1972–73 season was competent and solid, but far from experienced. Realizing that the core of any good hockey team was reliable goaltending, Fletcher had acquired the services of netminders Dan Bouchard and Phil Myre in the 1972 NHL expansion draft. Originally drafted by the Boston Bruins, Dan Bouchard had yet to play an NHL game when Atlanta selected him in the 1972 expansion draft. Myre, a former draft pick of the Montréal Canadiens, was the Flames' first selection.

To patrol the blue line in front of their two starting netminders, Fletcher and Geoffrion selected Kerry Ketter, Ron Harris and Randy Manery from the Red Wings, Bill Plager from the Blues, Pat Quinn from the Canucks and Larry Hale from the Flyers. As forwards, the Flames picked up wingers Norm Gratton from the Rangers, Larry Romanchych from the Blackhawks, Bill MacMillan from the Leafs, Keith McCreary from the Penguins, Lew Morrison from the Flyers, Lucien Grenier from the Kings, Bill Heindl from the North Stars and Frank Hughes from the California Golden Seals. Centering those forwards were Rod Zaine from the Sabres, Bob Leiter from the Penguins, Morris Stefiniw from the Rangers and Ernie Hick from the Seals. All together the Flames picked up 21 of the players existing NHL teams had left unprotected in the draft. All of them were capable of playing in the NHL, but none had wowed the league with their skill and finesse.

Recognizing that youth would play an important part in building a competitive franchise, Fletcher also went looking for raw talent in the 1972 Amateur Draft. Picking second in the draft,

Fletcher grabbed Quebéc Remparts center Jacques Richard. The speedy 20-year-old had fired up the Remparts' offense the previous season, tallying 71 goals and 89 assists for 160 points in 61 games. As skilled as he was, Richard also had a tough streak—he logged 100 penalty minutes that year.

Fletcher looked west for his second pick, drafting puck-moving defenseman Dwight Bialowas from the Regina Pats of the Western Canada Hockey League (WCHL) in the second round. He paired Bialowas with Sherbrooke Beavers defenseman Jean Lemieux as his third-round selection, then drafted right-winger Don Martineau from the New Westminster Bruins.

The team that took to the ice at the beginning of the 1972–73 season, Atlanta's first, was more workmanlike than talented. What the team lacked in finesse, however, it made up for in hard work.

The team played its first game as a franchise on October 7, 1972, against the New York Islanders with a sense of nervousness and excitement. After 60 minutes of play, the Atlanta Flames had accomplished what few expansion teams ever do— they scored a victory in their first match, downing the newly minted New York Islanders 3–2. Morris Stefaniw made history by scoring the team's first goal, shorthanded, at 12:48 in the first period. As he did, Manery was making history in the box, serving the team's first penalty for hooking.

That first win was not a sign of things to come once the Flames began battling more established, talented teams. They were beaten 5–3 by the Buffalo Sabres in their next game. That defeat started a five-game losing streak, interrupted only by a later 1–1 tie with the Sabres. The streak reached its lowest point in a 6–0 drubbing at the hands of the Minnesota North Stars. The second time Atlanta and Minnesota met, only three nights after the shutout, the Flames turned things around and skated home with a 3–2 victory.

For the rest of the season, the team managed to win or tie about as many games as it lost. At the end of their 78-game season, the Flames were eighth in the nine-team Western Division with a record of 25 wins, 38 losses and 15 ties. That respectable first-season finish was the direct result of some stellar goaltending on the part of Bouchard and Myre, who were left to stand on their heads some nights playing in Atlanta. Myre played 46 games and finished the year with a 3.04 goals-against average, posting three shutouts. Bouchard started in 34 games and managed to keep his goals-against average to an impressive 2.40. He posted two shutouts of his own.

Up front, the expansion draft pick Bob Leiter proved to critics he was worthy of his position as the Flames' top center, clocking in with a respectable season at the head of the Flames offense. He finished tops in scoring for the team, firing home 26 goals and assisting on 34 for 60 total points. Larry Romanchych finished behind Leiter for second place with 48 points. Rey Comeau and Keith McCreary each hit the 20-goal plateau, finishing third and fourth respectively in team scoring. Rookie Jacques Richard, who made the jump to the NHL from the Québec Major Junior Hockey League (QMJHL) in his rookie season, played 74 games for the team, tallying 13 goals and 18 assists for 31 points. Randy Manery and Pat Quinn anchored the blue line for the team, scoring 35 and 20 points respectively. Quinn proved to be the Flames tough guy, leading the team with 113 penalty minutes in his 78 games of regular season work.

The Flames played their 29 home games in front of respectable crowds, averaging just over 12,000 fans per night. Their fan support and their record were not enough, however, to guarantee the Flames a playoff spot in their first season. The team could take some solace in knowing they had finished 35 points ahead of their expansion sisters, the New York Islanders.

The first season hadn't even ended when Fletcher—who would later be nicknamed "Trader Cliff"—started swapping players to bring Arnie Brown, Leon Rochefort, Curt Bennett and Butch Deadmarsh to Atlanta. Fletcher was paying special attention to the upcoming draft, where the Flames would pick second overall. Although Richard's 31 points were good enough for a top-10 finish in team scoring, Fletcher had been counting on more production from his rookie. He wanted goals by the dozen from his young players, particularly from first-round draft picks.

So when the 1973 draft convened, Fletcher wasted no time in going after the players he wanted. The Islanders had the first pick in the draft and did what everyone expected, choosing Denis Potvin. The Flames were next and chose forward Tom Lysiak to be their next star. The 20-year-old from Alberta—who was also drafted 23rd overall by the WHA's Houston Aeros that same year—had been lighting up the WCHL as part of the Medicine Hat Tigers for the last three years. At the end of his draft year and after 67 games for the Tigers, Lysiak counted 58 goals and 96 assists for 154 points. He had also racked up 104 penalty minutes. Fletcher saw in Lysiak a goal scorer who could take care of himself on the ice and hoped Lysiak would be ready to make the jump from the minors into the pros as quickly as possible.

For the rest of the draft, Fletcher went fishing for talent, using the picks he had accumulated through trades during the regular season to bolster the team's depth. After taking New Westminster winger Vic Mercredi at the end of the first round, Fletcher pounced on Sudbury Wolves forward Eric Vail, who had scored 48 goals and 57 assists in the previous season. Fletcher knew that Vail needed some more experience at the minor pro level and assigned him to the Omaha Knights for the 1973–74 season. The relegation lasted only 37 games, and Vail returned to play with the Flames halfway through the year. Fletcher also decided to add some beef to his defensive corps, selecting defenseman Ken Houston from the Chatham Maroons with the 85th pick in the draft.

In training camp, Lysiak quickly proved that he was ready to move up from the minors and secured a spot on the team's opening-day roster. With Myre and Bouchard still holding their own between the pipes, the team charged up the standings in the West Division. With 30 wins, 34 losses and 4 ties, the team's record was under .500, but the Flames still finished 4th in the division and only four points behind the third-place Los Angeles Kings. The Atlanta Flames were going to the post-season for the first time in team history.

To capture the attention of the league, Lysiak had to play his best, and that's exactly what he did, scoring a team-leading 64 points with 19 goals and 45 assists. Despite his strong showing, Lysiak finished second in Calder Trophy voting behind Denis Potvin. Still, Fletcher and Geoffrion were impressed with what Lysiak had brought to the team. Bob Leiter finished behind Lysiak in team scoring with 26 goals and 26 assists. Larry Romanchych scored 22 goals, and the temperamental Richard potted 27 of his own. Thirty-seven games into the season, the team called up Vail from Omaha for a 23-game stint in which the youngster managed 2 goals and 9 assists. He also accumulated 30 penalty minutes.

Bouchard and Myre switched roles in their second season. As the new go-to goalie, Bouchard played in 46 games, posting 19 wins and managing a sparkling 2.77 goals-against average. He racked up five shutouts. Myre tended the twine in only 36 games, phoning in 11 wins and 16 losses without any shutouts. His goals-against average was 3.33.

The Flames' regular season record ensured the team a first-round match-up with the Philadelphia Flyers in the Stanley Cup playoffs. The Flyers had finished first in the west, one point shy of the Boston Bruins who finished first place overall in the NHL with 112 points. The game looked like a mismatch. If anyone thought the Flames stood any chance against the Flyers, they weren't very vocal about it.

The series opened up April 9 in the City of Brotherly Love with the Flyers romping to a 4–1 victory. Philly won the second game 5–1 two nights later. In what would later prove to be an odd turn of history, a young player named Terry Crisp who had been drafted only the year before and would become the Flames head coach years later, scored once against the Atlanta team. In game three the Flyers won 4–1, but the game lasted 40 minutes longer than anyone expected due to a brawl that broke out late in the game. The referee handed out a total of 132 penalty minutes because of the fiasco.

The win gave the Flyers a 3–0 series lead heading into game four. To everyone's surprise, Atlanta looked like they might actually be able to win the game and stretch the series to five games. Halfway through the second period, the Flames had piled up a 3–0 lead. Then the Flyers woke up. Philly scored three straight goals and notched the winner in overtime, sending the Flames to the golf course for the rest of the post-season.

Despite the early exit, the Flames had much to be excited about. Lysiak had come into his own as a rookie, and Vail was showing promise. Leiter and Romanchych were both pulling their weight as forwards, and Bouchard and Myre were providing steady goaltending on the backend. But Fletcher still wanted more offensive pop, and he went into the 1974 amateur draft intent on finding another goal scorer. Forced to wait until the second round, Fletcher decided to go with Québec Remparts forward Guy Chouinard who had lit up the QMJHL's best goaltenders with 75 goals and 85 assists in his draft year. Despite his offensive skill, the Flames assigned the youngster to their minor league for the bulk of the following season, save for a brief five-game call-up.

The Flames team that took to the ice at the beginning of the 1974–75 season was still led by Lysiak, Leiter and Quinn and looked much like it had the season before. But the team was ready to improve on its record from the previous two years and did, finishing the year with 34 wins, 31 ties and 15 ties, its first winning season.

Unfortunately, too many of the team's big names spent too much of the season battling injury. Leiter, Romanchych and Richard spent time on the trainer's table, which sapped the Flames' offensive potential. Then a nine-game losing streak between December 2 and December 22 drained away the momentum from what seemed destined to be an impressive season. The streak culminated late in the year with the resignation of Geoffrion as coach. Fred Creighton, the coach of the team's Tulsa affiliate, replaced him.

With Leiter off the ice for almost 30 games, Lysiak had stepped in to fill the void, pushing his offensive game to a new level by scoring 25 goals and 52 assists. Curt Bennett finished just behind Lysiak with 64 points of his own. The real surprise of the year, however, was rookie Eric Vail. The previous year, the young forward played only 23 games and scored only 11 points. But that year he lit up the NHL, scoring 39 goals and 21 assists for a total of 60 points. This offensive explosion was good enough to win Vail the Calder Trophy for rookie of the year.

Unfortunately, the Calder was the only piece of hardware the Flames had any chance of taking home. Although their winning record was impressive, it was not good enough for a slot in the post-season.

The next three seasons were essentially repeats of 1974–75. The Flames continued to improve marginally but struggled to find a winning formula in the post-season. In all three seasons, the Flames finished with a win-loss record either at or just above .500. In each season, Lysiak was first in team scoring with Vail typically finishing second or third. Both scored 30 goals at least twice. The only surprise addition to the Flames roster was 1975 draft pick Willi Plett, who broke into the league the following year with 33 goals, 23 assists and 123 penalty minutes. Plett's triumphant season gave the Flames their second Calder Trophy winner in three years.

The Flames backend, however, was starting to fail. Although the team scored 264 goals during the 1976–77 season, they also surrendered 265 to their opponents. Myre and Bouchard were still playing well, but their relationship was growing acrimonious as each began clamoring for more playing time.

The 1977–78 season saw some additional roster changes as Fletcher, tired of the conflict between his two goaltenders, traded Myre to the St. Louis Blues for goalie Yves Belanger, defenseman Dick Redmond and forward Bob MacMillan. The move cleared the way for Bouchard to take over as the starting goalie. He responded by racking up 25 wins in 58 games and a goals-against average of 2.75. MacMillan potted 31 goals for the team. Despite the improved play, the fans in Atlanta were losing interest. By the end of the regular season, the Flames' regular season attendance had plummeted from 12,000 to 10,000. What interest there was for hockey in Georgia was dwindling with every early playoff exit. The Flames needed to get momentum in the post-season, to win more than one game in a series and maybe punch their way into the second or third rounds.

During the three tough seasons, this had not been happening. The Flames' post-season bad luck would not go away even with the coaching change and Plett's addition to the team. The Los Angeles Kings bounced the Flames from the play-offs in both 1975–76 and 1976–77. Of the five total playoff games the two teams played against one another in those two seasons, the Flames won only once. In 1977–78, the Detroit Red Wings took on the role of spoiler, pushing the Flames out of the post-season.

In 1978–79, the team took some dramatic steps forward. For the first time, someone other than Lysiak led in scoring. MacMillan beat him, recording 37 goals and 71 assists for 108 points. Draft pick Guy Chouinard finished second with 107 points and became the first Flame ever to score 50 goals in a season. Eric Vail scored 83 points of his own. The team finished with a record of 41 wins, 31 losses and 8 ties and a team-high 90 points. Unfortunately, even this solid finish in the regular season didn't give the Flames the momentum they needed to get past the first round of the playoffs. The team dropped two straight games against the Toronto Maple Leafs in their best-of-three series, making yet another early exit.

Fletcher knew it was time to make some significant changes and decided to start at the top. Now team president as well as general manager, Fletcher replaced head coach Fred Creighton with a close personal friend, former Montréal Canadiens coach Al MacNeil. Fletcher also started looking for players to jump-start his team and went into the 1979 draft intent on building a team for the future. He drafted defenseman Paul Reinhart in the first round. In subsequent rounds, he picked up goaltender Pat Riggin and forwards Tim Hunter and Jim Peplinski. It would prove to be one of the Flames' best drafting years ever as all four players became regulars on the Flames squad.

Meanwhile, the WHA had finally folded, and its demise meant that Winnipeg, Edmonton, Québec and Hartford were granted NHL franchises. The deal that granted these teams admission to the NHL guaranteed that NHL teams could reclaim players from the WHA for whom they held the playing rights. Fletcher dipped into the pool and pulled Swedish winger Kent Nilsson, a gifted skater and scorer, back from the Winnipeg Jets. Unfortunately, his nickname— "The Magic Man"—referred to both his skill and a propensity for disappearing on game night.

Not even the addition of Nilsson could break the Atlanta Flames' post-season bad luck. Nilsson led the team in scoring with 40 goals and 53 assists, and Chouinard backed him with 31 goals of his own. Paul Reinhart managed 9 goals and 38 assists as a rookie. The Flames' regular season record, however, dropped to 35 wins, 32 losses and 13 ties and a total of 83 points. Atlanta did manage to beat the New York Rangers 4–2 in game three of their first-round series. This win doubled the franchise's total playoff wins. But the Rangers won games one, two and four, bouncing the Flames once again from the post-season.

The last game the Flames played at the Omni on April 12, 1980, turned out to be a 5–2 loss to the Rangers. With attendance dwindling and a lack of post-season revenue to make up the losses, the owners of the Atlanta Flames quietly began shopping the team around the league. The team had lasted an astounding seven seasons and become competitive, but there was nothing left to gain from leaving the team where it was. Georgia was not the hockey hotbed the owners had hoped it would be.

Late on the evening of April 12, the rink attendants closed and locked the doors of the Omni behind the departing players for the last time.

Chapter Two

Alberta Bound

When the Atlanta Flames were put up for sale at the end of the 1979–80 season, a group of businessmen in Calgary, Alberta, took notice and began to pool their resources to buy the team.

The potential buyers had very different backgrounds. Norman Green was a Calgary developer and pillar of the community who had participated in the reconstruction of several of the city's historical buildings. Harley Hotchkiss was an accomplished oilman and a real estate developer. Norman Kwong was a sales and leasing negotiator with Knowlton Realty who had also played for the Canadian Football League's Edmonton Eskimos, dubbing himself "the greatest Chinese fullback of all time." Ralph Scurfield, CEO of Nu-West Group, also threw his hat into the ownership ring with his brothers Byron J. (BJ) and Daryl "Doc" Seaman. This unlikely group began negotiating quietly with Cousins in Atlanta and, before long, had secured a deal to buy the team.

Calgary was an ideal place for a hockey team. Nestled in the foothills of the great Rocky Mountains, it was a Canadian city whose winters were cold and snowy. So the climate was right. The city was increasingly the home to key players in the oil industry, who were reaping millions in dollars of profits from oil exploration in Alberta. So there was plenty of money to support a team. But most importantly, Calgary's residents wanted a professional hockey team to call their own.

During the abbreviated run of the WHA in the 1970s, the city had tried repeatedly to make a go of professional hockey. The league had envisioned a great inter-provincial battle between a Calgary team and an Edmonton franchise. But running a team under the WHA proved to be problematic. Although the city was granted one of the league's 10 original franchises, the Calgary Broncos, the team never took to the ice. Owner Bob Brownridge had become ill and missed a $10,000 payment due to the league. Rather than wait for it to arrive, the WHA yanked the team out of Calgary before the season even started.

Three years later, the city joined the WHA again. This time, rather than building a franchise from the ground up, the city went looking for an existing team that was looking for a new place to play. That team was the WHA's Vancouver Blazers.

The Blazers had originally joined the league as the Miami Screaming Eagles, but cash flow problems and the lack of a suitable arena forced the team to move to Philadelphia before their first season. Once there, the team, now dubbed the Philadelphia Blazers, discovered they couldn't compete with the NHL's Philadelphia Flyers for attendance and revenue. So, at the end of the 1973 season, their first in the city, they pulled up stakes and moved north of the border to Vancouver. For the next two seasons, the Blazers played out of Vancouver's Pacific Coliseum. Their first season there was abysmal as the team finished with a record of 27 wins, 50 losses and 1 tie. In the second season, they finished only two games below .500, a respectable showing. But the improvement didn't generate enough fan interest to keep the team in the city. Following the 1974–75 season, the Blazers once again packed up and moved, this time to Calgary.

Rebranded the Calgary Cowboys, the team played its home games out of the 7200-seat Stampede Corral. In their first season, they skated to a record of 41 wins, 35 losses and 4 ties, qualifying for the playoffs. Unfortunately, their first-round match against the Québec Nordiques proved more memorable for the on-ice brawling than the quality of the play. During one game, Cowboys enforcer Rick Jodzio attacked Québec Nordiques player Marc Tardif, causing a major head trauma and forcing Tardif out of the series. A bench-clearing brawl resulted, and Jodzio later pleaded guilty to a criminal charge that resulted in a court-ordered fine and suspension from play.

With Tardif off the ice, the Cowboys went on to defeat the Nordiques in five games. They next ran into the solid, fast-skating Winnipeg Jets, a team they simply couldn't handle, and were ejected from the playoffs.

Despite the Cowboys' first-season success, no one in Calgary seemed interested in the team. Although the Corral was small, it was seldom full and rumors began to fly that the team might move to Ottawa. By this time the WHA was in full freefall. Across the league, teams were folding or moving to new cities as soon as they were set up. Ottawa had already seen a franchise, the Ottawa Nationals, come and go. There just seemed to be little appetite for non-NHL professional hockey.

During the Cowboys' second year at Calgary, attendance dwindled, and the quality of play nosedived. The Cowboys missed the playoffs with a record of 31 wins, 43 losses and 7 ties. When it became clear that the Cowboys were not going to be able to sell enough season tickets to make the 1977–78 season worthwhile, management abandoned the franchise. As of May 31, 1977, the Cowboys no longer existed, and Calgary was without a hockey team.

Three years later, with the purchase of the Atlanta Flames pending, Calgary seemed ready to give professional hockey another shot, this time as part of the NHL. There was, however, one unresolved issue that was holding up the purchase. On average, modern NHL rinks seated approximately 15,000 people. Compared to this standard, Calgary's Stampede Corral was far from adequate. Luckily, the city had been awarded the 1988 Winter Olympics. When the Alberta government learned of the Calgary group's ambition to buy the Atlanta Flames, it asked the group to hold off on finalizing the deal until it could decide how much money to invest in building the event sites. One of them, a full-sized arena, might serve as the Flames' new home.

In this moment of uncertainty, Nelson Skalbania stepped in and forced the potential buyers to finish off the deal.

A native of British Columbia, Skalbania, was well known in the business world for his rapid-fire real estate deals. A real estate mogul, he was the master of the quick flip, acquiring properties and then selling them off quickly for a profit.

Since owning a hockey team was neither a quick nor a sure-fire way to make money, especially in Canada, Skalbania's interest in the Flames was surprising. A franchise's operating costs suck up the bulk of gate revenues, meaning commercial promotions and TV contracts have to generate the profits. Owning a team and making it profitable requires staying power as well as planning, two traits that were not Skalbania's strengths.

Yet, Skalbania had already dipped into the world of sports ownership more than once and with spectacular results. In 1976–77, he had purchased the WHA's Edmonton Oilers for approximately $300,000. At the time of the purchase, the Oilers were saddled with approximately $1.6 million in debt. Skalbania turned around and, over a late night dinner at an Edmonton steakhouse, signed over half of the team and their debt to his close friend Peter Pocklington in exchange for a Rolls Royce, a diamond ring and a painting, together worth approximately $700,000. Within a year, Skalbania had signed over the rest of the team to Pocklington.

Rather than leave the business of sports ownership to those with the patience for it, Skalbania immediately acquired ownership rights to the WHA's Indianapolis Racers. Although the Racers did not last as a franchise, Skalbania left a permanent mark on the world of professional hockey when, in 1978, he signed a young Brantford, Ontario player named Wayne Gretzky to a personal services contract, which he later sold to Pocklington.

According to Calgary Flames' lore, Skalbania, who was always looking for a good business opportunity, became interested in the Flames while honeymooning in Greece. He learned that Cousins was looking to move the Flames out of Atlanta and called his daughter in Canada. He told her to go to Atlanta and offer to buy the team.

"I told her: 'Take an offer for a million dollars, get on a plane and go down to Atlanta," Skalbania later said. "She was, oh, 17 or 18 at the time. Here I was, lying on a Greek beach, trying to buy a hockey team."

Apparently, Skalbania's daughter arrived in Atlanta shortly thereafter and met with team president Cliff Fletcher. But according to Fletcher, her offer was not typical of how business was done in the real world.

"I knew Nelson, of course, but I had no idea who *she* was or what she was doing there. And she had the offer on a cocktail napkin. I swear, on a cocktail napkin," Fletcher said.

The group of Calgary businessmen was stunned by Skalbania's offer, especially since he had no personal ties to the community, but they were not discouraged. Rather than abandon their bid, they sat down with Skalbania and hammered out a deal that allowed Skalbania to buy a 50 percent stake in the team. The original ownership group divided the rest among themselves. In all, they offered Cousins $16 million for the purchase of the Flames, the largest sum ever offered for an NHL franchise. Cousins snapped up the deal. In the 1980–81 season, the Atlanta Flames would play in Calgary. It was the first and only time an NHL team would move from the United States to Canada.

The ownership group quickly asked the public what to name the team. Since Calgary was located in the heart of farming and cattle country and was the host city of North America's largest stampede, many of the early suggestions revolved around western themes. The Mustangs and the Spurs were early suggestions. Some suggested resurrecting the Cowboys as a team name. Another popular idea involved naming the team the Chinooks for the warm winds that swept out of the Rocky Mountains in the middle of winter.

In the end, the public decided not to tamper with the team's identity and allowed the Flames to stand as the team's name. A flaming "C" replaced the flaming "A," and the team kept their red and white colors.

In the beginning, the Calgary Flames looked like something from the days of the frontier. The entire franchise—the players, the coach, even Cliff Fletcher—pulled up stake and moved to Calgary, where they operated out of several trailers located in the middle of Stampede Park. Their stadium, the Stampede Corral, was still considered too small for an NHL team to call home, but the Flames' stay there would be temporary. The Alberta government had voted to spend millions of dollars to build a new arena for the Olympics, and construction began quickly. After the games, the Calgary Olympic Coliseum would be renamed the Saddledome, a reference to the roof's swooping shape, which resembled a western horse saddle.

The team that took to the ice for its first game on October 9, 1980, was different from the Atlanta team of the previous year. The biggest change was in the Flames' net. Draft pick Pat Riggin and free agent Rejean Lemelin quickly supplanted Dan Bouchard as the team's go-to goalies. Tom Lysiak was gone, traded during the 1978–79 season to the Chicago Blackhawks.

In 1977, Pat Quinn had retired. Paul Reinhart took Quinn's spot on defense, and draft pick Jim Peplinski took up a regular playing position on the forward unit. Kevin Lavalee, drafted out of Brantford in the second round of the summer's amateur draft, also made the team.

The core of the team remained intact, however. Kent Nilsson was now the anchor for the Flames offense, followed by forwards Guy Chouinard, Willi Plett, Eric Vail and Bob MacMillan. The combination gave the Flames a potent offensive corps that would hopefully score more goals than their new goaltenders would allow their opponents.

The buzz in Calgary for the start of the Flames season was much greater than what had been for the Cowboys of the WHA. Fans snapped up season tickets as soon as they went on sale, and soon, every single season seat was sold. The city embraced its new team, and every home game the team played that year in the diminutive Corral was sold out.

On October 9, 1980, when the Flames took to the ice to play the Québec Nordiques in their first game in their new home, the Corral was packed to the rafters. The game ended in a 5–5 tie. The Flames dropped their next game 6–2 to the Colorado Rockies and then tied the Blackhawks 3–3 in their third game. But they finally notched a win on October 14, beating the Los Angeles Kings 4–2.

Despite a slow start, the Flames proved to be an offensive juggernaut in their first season, scoring at least 10 goals in three separate games. They beat the Detroit Red Wings 10–0 and the Edmonton Oilers 10–4. Against the New York Islanders, they scored an astonishing 11–4 victory. The three lopsided wins helped spur the Flames on to a winning record in their inaugural season in the NHL. The team finished with a record of 39 wins, 27 losses and 14 ties. In front of their new fans in their tiny rink, the Flames played well enough to finish in third place in the Patrick Division and to earn a playoff spot.

Continuing his regular season magic, Kent Nilsson led the Flames in scoring with 49 goals, 82 assists and 131 points, finishing third place in the league behind the Oilers' Wayne Gretzky and the Kings' Marcel Dionne. Guy Chouinard continued to show that his underperforming rookie years were ancient history, scoring 31 goals and 52 assists. Willi Plett scored 38 goals of his own, and Eric Vail and Bob MacMillan bulged the twine 28 times each. Don Lever, a newcomer from the Vancouver Canucks, chipped in 26 goals. Paul Reinhart continued to prove he could move the puck as well as anyone on the ice, scoring 18 goals and 49 assists for 67 points, a respectable total for a defenseman.

Although Dan Bouchard had been a fixture in the Flames' net since the team's inception in Atlanta, moving to Calgary proved overwhelming for the perennial first-string Flames goaltender. In 14 games, Bouchard posted the worst goals-against average of his career— 4.03—winning only four games that year. With youngsters Pat Riggin and Rejean Lemelin starting to show they could play at the elite level of the NHL, Fletcher traded Bouchard to the Québec Nordiques for forward Jamie Hislop halfway through the season. Hislop would go on to score 15 points in 29 games for Calgary.

With Bouchard out of the picture, Riggin picked up the slack in goal, starting in 42 games for the Flames, winning 21 and posting a 3.83 goals-against average. Lemelin saw action in 29 games of his own, sporting a rock solid record of 14 wins, 6 losses and 7 ties. He posted a 3.24 goals-against average with two shutouts. Allowing fewer than three goals per game was now a thing of the past for most NHL goalies. Led by the Edmonton Oilers, teams were focusing first and foremost on offense, and more often than not, their goaltenders were left to fend for themselves.

Calgary's strong regular season earned them a home-ice faceoff against the Chicago Blackhawks in the opening round of the playoffs. The night of the match, the Corral was packed with fans who knew the Flames' post-season woes in Atlanta and wondered if they could somehow reverse their playoff fortunes in Calgary. The Flames gave them reason to cheer, sweeping Chicago in three straight games 4–3, 6–2 and 5–4. In this one charge, the Flames had posted more playoff victories than they had accumulated in their entire history and their first-ever series win.

Unfortunately, the celebrations didn't last very long. The win set the Flames on a collision course with the Philadelphia Flyers, who had finished five points ahead of them that year. The Broadstreet Bullies were a tough, physical and highly skilled team, but the Flames weren't being intimidated. The Flames dropped the first game in Philadelphia 4–0 but then came back for a 5–4 win in the next game to take the series home to Calgary. There the Flames wowed their fans, winning game three 2–1 and game four 5–4. Heading back to Pennsylvania with a 3–1 series lead, the Flames needed only one win to knock out the Flyers.

Philadelphia didn't cooperate, and in their worst drubbing of the season, the Flames lost the fifth game by a score of 9–4. Back home in Calgary for game six, the Flames dropped a 3–2 squeaker to even the series at three games apiece.

Two nights later, playing again in Philadelphia, the Flames etched out a decisive 4–1 win, thanks to the help of some brilliant goaltending by Pat Riggin, and took the series.

The Atlanta Flames had never won a playoff series. In their first-ever post-season, the Calgary Flames had won two. One more would put them in the Stanley Cup final. But to earn a chance at the Cup, they had to get past the Minnesota North Stars. Unfortunately, the Flames were tired from their seven-game tilt with the Flyers and never quite caught up to the North Stars. Although the Flames made a series of it, posting 3–2 and 3–1 wins on home ice, the North Stars went on to win four games, eliminating Calgary from the playoffs

The Flames' first post-season in their new home had given the players and their fans cause for optimism. Pat Riggin had proven he was as capable as any other goaltender currently in the league, and Guy Chouinard, who scored 3 goals and 14 assists in 16 games, had proven he was a true playoff performer. But there was still something missing from the team, and Fletcher decided it was time to go looking for it. He quickly found it. But as soon as he did, the Calgary Flames began to come apart.

Chapter Three

Growing Pains in Cowtown

The Flames' first season in Calgary was a success. Not only had they had made it to the playoffs, they had won two series decisively, showing their fans and the rest of the league that they were able to compete. But the loss to the Minnesota North Stars had shown that there was still work to do. The Flames were good, but they weren't good enough.

Part of the problem was the Flames' defense. They were a solid unit, but the rest of the league was catching on to the Edmonton Oilers' firebrand, go-for-the-jugular offensive approach to hockey. To hold back this new style of attack, Fletcher knew he needed to add more to his blue line. So at the 1981 entry draft, with 15th overall pick in the first round, Fletcher selected Kitchener Rangers defenseman Al MacInnis.

A native of Inverness, Nova Scotia, MacInnis had raised eyebrows while playing at the junior hockey level. In only his second season in the Ontario Hockey League (OHL), the youngster tallied 25 goals and 50 assists. He also racked up 145 penalty minutes while playing on the Rangers backend. The youngster was known for his accurate passing, his sound defensive game and his deadly slapshot.

With goaltenders Pat Riggin and Reggie Lemelin now playing in the big leagues, Fletcher knew he also had to start preparing for the future between the pipes. In the third round of the draft, he pulled a player from the Flames' own backyard, drafting puckstopper Mike Vernon, who had tended goal for the WHL's Calgary Wranglers the previous two years. The Calgary-born, 5'9" Vernon had posted winning records in both of his two seasons with goals-against averages of 3.77 and 3.68.

With construction of the Flames' new arena well underway and a successful post-season run behind them, the fans in Calgary returned at the beginning of the 1981–82 season with high hopes. But their expectations proved difficult to meet. After tying the Vancouver Canucks 1–1 in their season opener, then beating the St. Louis Blues 6–4 two nights later, the Flames quickly unravelled. Playing what would be the worst hockey seen in the city of Calgary for years, the Flames won only two of their next 17 games.

Although some of the games were close, too many were lopsided thrashings. The Oilers beat the Flames 8–4. In a 12–4 loss to the Detroit Red Wings, the Flames surrendered more goals than it had in any other game in the team's history. They were spanked by the Chicago Blackhawks 10–4, only to receive a 7–0 drubbing two nights later at the hands of the St. Louis Blues. Although no team could play perfectly every night, this streak was unacceptable. The Flames needed to play better, and Fletcher knew it.

"The problem was—and we knew it right then—Edmonton was building one of the greatest teams to play the game in a heck of a long time. And the players who had spent time in Atlanta had a lot of trouble adjusting to Calgary," said Fletcher. "Because Calgary is a Canadian city, and because of what was happening to the north of us in Edmonton, there was a lot of pressure on our team to win. And the players we had in Atlanta didn't like that pressure."

"Trader Cliff" promptly began working deals to get rid of players who were having problems adjusting to life in Cowtown. Fletcher traded defenseman Brad Marsh to the Philadelphia Flyers for scoring center Mel Bridgman. When that trade failed to produce any immediate change, Fletcher pulled the trigger again. What followed would begin one of the greatest chapters in Flames history.

With just over 20 games gone in the season, Fletcher put in a call to the Colorado Rockies to inquire about one of their forwards, a mustache-sporting Alberta-born player named Lanny McDonald.

Born in Hanna, Alberta, in 1953, McDonald had entered the NHL playing in one of professional sports' most pressure-packed markets. After six games for the Calgary Centennials in 1970–71, McDonald switched to the Medicine Hat Tigers and lit up the rest of the WCHL. In 136 junior games, McDonald scored 112 goals and 141 assists for 253 points—nearly two points per game! The Toronto Maple Leafs took notice and chose McDonald as the fourth overall draft pick in the 1973 draft.

Unlike most young draft picks, McDonald required no seasoning at the minor pro level. He made the jump to the big club in his first year, playing 70 games and scoring 14 goals and 16 assists. After the 1973–74 season, in which he scored 44 points, McDonald attacked the NHL with a vengeance. In 1974–75, he broke through the 30-goal plateau putting 37 points on the board and helping out with 56 assists. The following season, he upped the ante, potting 46 goals and making 44 assists. In each of the next three years with the Leafs, McDonald scored at least 40 goals.

Despite McDonald's scoring prowess, the Leafs of the 1970s were an average team generating average results. Punch Imlach ran the team at the time with sometimes questionable decision-making skills: he traded away Leafs legends Daryl Sittler and Tiger Williams, for example. On December 29, 1979, Imlach shipped both Lanny McDonald and Joel Quenneville to the Colorado Rockies in a trade for wingers Pat Hickey and Wilf Paiement.

Rather than sulk over his misfortune, McDonald played hockey and played it well. In 46 games with the Rockies, McDonald scored 25 goals. Combined with the 15 he'd scored with the Leafs, he once again posted 40 goals for the season.

The following season McDonald dropped to only 35 goals, but he could hardly be blamed for it. The Rockies were a bad hockey team, winning only 19 games in 1979–80 and only 22 games in 1980–81. Since its inception as a franchise, the team had always sat at the bottom of the league. Even at 35 goals, McDonald's performance on forward was one of the team's few bright spots.

But losses on the ice became losses in the crowds. The franchise was coming apart and the 1981–82 season would prove to be the Rockies' last. When Fletcher approached the team about a possible trade—McDonald for Bob MacMillan and Don Lever—it was the perfect opportunity to get the young scorer off a sinking ship. The Rockies took the trade and sent their star to Calgary.

In addition to scoring prowess, McDonald brought experience and leadership to the team. He had been playing in the NHL for eight years and knew what it took to win. He played as hard as he could every single night, setting a positive example for the rest of the team. His arrival in Calgary had an instant effect on the team. The trade happened on November 25, 1981. Of the 11 games that followed, the Flames lost only three.

Not everyone on the Flames roster got a boost from McDonald's arrival in Calgary. For most of the season, tension had been brewing in the team's locker room. Players such as Willi Plett and Pat Riggin, two of the team's most important skaters, were openly thumbing their noses at coach Al MacNeil and assistant coach Pierre Page. On one occasion, a reporter watching Page put the Flames through their paces during practice saw Riggin throw a stick at the coach. Later that year, MacNeil benched Plett for a game. Apparently, the forward had laughed during a team meeting when MacNeil gave instructions.

The dissension in the ranks was visible on the scoreboard.

The Flames had a poor start for the season and never recovered. They finished the year with a losing record of 29 wins, 34 losses and 17 ties, scoring a lowly 75 points. But since their record was better than that of the Colorado Rockies and the Los Angeles Kings, the Flames finished third behind the Oilers and the Vancouver Canucks in the Smythe Division.

Their regular season record also earned the team a post-season match against the Canucks. But by this time the dissension that had disrupted the team locker room was overflowing onto the ice. In a departure from their previous post-season wins, the Flames returned to their "Flame-out" ways, dropping a best-of-five series to the Canucks in three straight games.

Chouinard led the team in scoring for the year with 23 goals and 57 assists for 80 points. But McDonald put more pucks into the goal, bulging the twine 34 times. Despite their losing record, it wasn't a bad year overall for the Flames as three players—McDonald, Jim Peplinski and Kevin LaVallee—scored at least 30 goals. Five others—Chouinard, Mel Bridgman, Willi Plett, Kent Nilsson and Ken Houston—all broached the 20-goal mark. Nilsson's separated shoulder had hit the Flames in the one spot they really needed production—goals. He ended up missing almost 40 regular season games. Paul Reinhart continued to quarterback the team's defense but also managed to rack up 68 points, which placed him third in scoring. Plett took his frustration with MacNeil out on opposing players, finishing the year with 288 penalty minutes.

It was time for a change, and Fletcher knew the biggest one needed to happen at the top. During the off-season, Fletcher shunted MacNeil into an administrative role, which amounted to firing him as head coach. The move was difficult for Fletcher. He and MacNeil had known one another for decades and were close friends. No one, however, was safe once Fletcher set out to repair the team.

Willi Plett and Pat Riggin were next to go. The season was barely over when, on June 7, Fletcher sent Plett and a fourth-round draft pick to Minnesota in a trade that brought Steve Christoff and Bill Nyrop to Calgary, and that secured the Flames a second-round pick in that year's draft. On June 9, Fletcher shipped Riggin and Ken Houston off to Washington. In exchange he got Howard Walker, George White, a sixth-round pick in the 1982 draft, a third-round pick in the 1983 draft and a second-round pick in the 1984 draft. After getting rid of the team problems, Fletcher sought to add some more veteran leadership to the team.

In September, he traded a pair of draft picks to the Montréal Canadiens for former first-round draft pick Doug Risebrough. Although known for his scoring touch at the junior hockey level, in the NHL the center had established himself as a hard-checking forward.

Unfortunately for Fletcher, the 1982 draft proved to be a total bust for the Flames. Without a first-round pick, Calgary had to wait until the second round to start making its selections. Few of the players that were left saw any ice time in the NHL. The Flames' second-round pick, Dave Reierson of Prince Albert, played in only two games for the team. The Flames' fourth-round pick, Mark Lamb, would eventually play over 400 games in the NHL, but only two of those were with Calgary. The rest of the team's selections—third-round defenseman Jim Laing and 12th-round pick Dale Thompson, among others—never saw a minute of regular season NHL play.

Other teams emerged from the draft with future superstars. Brian Bellows went to Minnesota, Scott Stevens to Washington, Ron Sutter to Philadelphia and his brother Rich Sutter to Pittsburgh. In addition, nine of the players drafted by other teams eventually went on to play for the Flames. Goaltender Ken Wregget went to Toronto; defenseman Phil Housley went to Buffalo; forward Michel Petit went to

Vancouver; Corey Millen went to the New York Rangers; Richard Kromm went to the New York Islanders; Craig Coxe went to Detroit; Dean Evanson went to Washington; Gary Leeman went to Toronto; and Doug Gilmour went to St. Louis. Of these, only Gilmour and Housley had any lasting effect on the Flames.

Without any substantial injection of youth into the lineup, the Flames had to make-do with what they had. The players as a corps were solid; they just needed the right leadership to take them to the next level. Fletcher had already hired Bob "Badger" Johnson to fill MacNeil's post. Badger was an accomplished hockey coach who had three U.S. college championships under his belt at the University of Wisconsin-Madison. The Minnesota-born, Korean War combat veteran also coached the 1976 U.S. Olympic hockey team and the United States' 1981 entry in the Canada Cup. But few Canadians knew who he was.

Johnson started out in hockey as a player, but his career stalled in university, and he had never taken to the ice as a professional. He first coached at Roosevelt High School in Minneapolis. A careful student of the game, he spent time studying and analyzing it from the perspective of an observer. He was a sound tactician and a perpetual optimist, always focusing on what players did right rather than what they did wrong, even after particularly bad games. Johnson's favorite expression was soon echoing across North American hockey rinks: "It's a great day for hockey!"

Given the upheaval on the team during the off-season, a period of adjustment was to be expected, and indeed, the 1982–83 season started off on a rocky note. The Flames dropped their first three games to the Edmonton Oilers, the New York Islanders and the Los Angeles Kings. However, only one week after dropping their first game, the Flames thrashed the Oilers in the second round of what was being dubbed by the media as "the Battle of Alberta" by a score of 9–4. For the rest of the season, the Flames gave as good as they got, trading wins and losses on a relatively even keel. The team finished the year with 32 wins, 34 losses and 14 ties, which was marginally better than their previous year's finish.

With Riggin gone from goal, Lemelin split the bulk of the playing time with newcomer Don Edwards, a netminder originally drafted by the Buffalo Sabres in 1975 (Edwards had goaltended on February 24, 1982, when Wayne Gretzky scored his record-breaking 77th goal, the most goals ever scored by a player in one season). Lemelin and Edwards chalked up 16 wins, despite their relatively sub-par goals-against averages of 3.61 and 4.02 respectively. Youngster Mike Vernon showed up in only five periods in two games but surrendered 11 goals, finishing the season with a goals-against average of 6.60.

With Nilsson back in the regular lineup and Lanny McDonald geared-up in red and white, the Flames started scoring goals by the bucketful. With this new offensive approach to the game, Lemelin and Edwards were often left to fend for themselves in the net. McDonald had a stellar season that captured the attention of his teammates, his opponents and the Calgary fans. In 80 games, he scored 66 times, a team record and a personal best. His final goal-scoring total was the second highest in the league and only five behind Wayne Gretzky's league-leading 71. Despite McDonald's strong showing, Nilsson led the team in scoring with 46 goals and 58 assists for a total 104 points. McDonald scored 32 assists, finishing the year just shy of 100 points. Paul Reinhart popped in 75 points in 78 games from the backend but also started playing some time at forward. Guy Chouinard chipped in 72 points of his own in a full season of work. In his debut year in the Flames' uniform, newcomer Doug Risebrough served up 21 goals and 37 assists for 58 points. He also collected 138 penalty minutes, the team high.

Although they finished below .500 for the second straight season, the Flames 78-point total was good enough for a second-place finish in the Smythe Division behind the Edmonton Oilers and a spot in the playoffs.

The Flames' first-round opponents were the Vancouver Canucks. The Canucks had finished only three points behind the Flames in regular season play, but they had lost five of the eight regular season games they'd played against Calgary. One was an 8–1 pasting on March 1. The first round turned out to be more of the same. Badger Bob deployed his team to meet the Canucks, and though Vancouver prevented a sweep by winning game three of the series, the Flames soundly beat them. Calgary took game one with a score of 4–3, game two with a score of 5–3 and game four with a score of 4–3.

If the first round seemed like a repeat of a regular season match-up, the second round was pure hockey history. The Oilers were the up-and-coming darlings of the league, sporting a lineup peppered with future superstars like Wayne Gretzky, Mark Messier and Kevin Lowe. Although separated by only 215 miles, the two cities considered themselves to be completely different from one another. When they met on the ice, their skill, aggressive play and outright hatred for each other made the Battle of Alberta one of the NHL's greatest rivalries. But the Flames and the Oilers had never before faced off in the playoffs.

Even though their lineup was deep, in the 1983 playoffs the Flames didn't stand a chance against the Oilers' fire wagon brand of hockey. The series was a massacre. Gretzky, Messier, Coffey, Anderson and the rest of the Oilers lit up the Flames for 34 goals over five games. They took the first two games in Edmonton by scores of 6–3 and 5–1 before humiliating the Flames in front of a packed Corral, beating them 10–2. Calgary managed to salvage some of its pride by beating the Oilers in the next Calgary game 6–5, but Edmonton responded two nights later with another offensive onslaught, pounding the Flames 9–1 to wrap up the series in five games.

The Oilers would go on to face the three-time Stanley Cup–champion New York Islanders in the final but would come up short against the hardened champs.

It wasn't all bad news for Calgary. At the end of the year, Lanny McDonald received the Bill Masterson Trophy, which is awarded to the player who best exemplified the qualities of perseverance, sportsmanship and dedication to the game of hockey.

Calgary fans could also look forward to a reward for their devotion. The April 18 game in which the Flames had beat the Oilers 6–5 was also the last game the team would ever play in the old Stampede Corral. Beginning in September, the team would play in its new digs at the Calgary Olympic Coliseum, already dubbed "the Saddledome."

Chapter Four

The More Things Change...

The Saddledome was one of many multi-million dollar construction projects built to prepare Calgary for the influx of international athletes, tourists and media expected for the 16-day sporting extravaganza that would be the 1988 Winter Olympics. It was also among the most expensive. Organizers pumped $72 million into Canada Olympic Park, a bobsleigh/luge/ski jump facility in the city's northwest end, and $5.9 million into a housing complex for the hundreds of international media who would be covering the event. Building the Saddledome cost $100 million: $29.7 million came from the federal government, $31.5 million from the city and province and $5 million from the Calgary Olympic Committee. In 1983, $100 million could buy you a lot of space, and space is what the organizers of the 1988 Winter Olympics and the Calgary Flames management had in mind when construction began in 1981.

The Saddledome was to be unique among NHL arenas because it could accommodate either an NHL-sized rink or an Olympic-sized rink, which is longer and wider than the ice used in North America. When an Olympic-sized playing sheet was needed, the first 14 rows of seats could retract, making room for more ice.

There was more space for spectators as well because the shape of the roof—an inverted hyperbolic parabola—meant there was more seating available at center ice. In all, the rink could house approximately 17,000 spectators. It offered 72 luxury boxes, two super suites, six restaurants and bars and myriad concession stands, souvenir stands and bathrooms.

The Flames had spent three seasons playing in front of 6000 fans. Now with new digs, they could make three times that number "ooh" and "ahh." But before the hockey season began, they needed to take care of the NHL amateur draft.

Picking 13th overall, the Flames dipped into the OHL and selected center Dan Quinn, who had scored 59 goals and 88 assists in 70 games in his draft year with the Belleville Bulls. The Flames had no second-round pick but could make two third-round choices. They wasted their first, picking London Knights center Brian Bradley. Then in the 55th overall pick of the draft, they selected the 6'2", Edmonton-born, St. Albert Saints center Perry Berezan. However, Berezan enrolled in the University of North Dakota at the beginning of the 1983–84 season, so his services would be a few years in coming.

The rest of the draft was a wasted exercise for Fletcher, who picked as diligently as he could but came away with little more in the way of professional talent. With the draft winding down into the 12th round and the best available players long since taken, Fletcher decided to take a gamble, selecting a Russian superstar by the name of Sergei Makarov.

In the early 1980s, drafting Russian players was widely considered a waste because it was nearly impossible to get them out of their country. During the Cold War, the Soviet Union was a closed Communist society and it kept a close eye on its citizens, limiting travel to Western nations as much as possible.

But hockey was as much a part of winter life in Russia as it was in Canada, and Makarov was already one of the game's rising stars. Twenty-five years old when the Flames drafted him, Makarov was a standout forward for the CSKA club team in Moscow. Much of his success had to do with his linemates Igor Larionov and Vladimir Krutov. Together the three formed a troika known locally and internationally as the KLM

Line or the Green Line. In 46 games during the 1981–82 season, Makarov scored 32 goals and 43 assists for 75 points. In his draft year, he scored 25 goals and 17 assists in only 30 games.

Makarov was also becoming a star on the international scene. He had been a member of the Soviet's gold medal–winning world junior teams in 1977 and 1978. After his second appearance, he was selected as the tournament's most valuable player. He had also played on the 1980 Soviet Olympic team that won a silver medal in Lake Placid, had patrolled the right wing for the Soviet's winning entry in the 1981 Canada Cup and had played for World Championship teams in 1979, 1981, 1982 and 1983. He was a rugged, talented player graced with incredible skating ability. He was also unlikely to receive permission to play in the NHL.

With the draft complete, the Flames set their mind on their playing. The Calgary team that took to the ice at the beginning of the 1983–84 season sported some attention-grabbing changes. The most important was that Hakan Loob, a young Swede who had decided to cross the Atlantic Ocean to attend training camp and had performed well there, chose to stick with the team as a winger. Defenseman Jamie Macoun, a free agent signed out of Ohio State who had seen action in only a handful of games the previous season, was also on the ice. Draft pick Dan Quinn had been reluctantly sent back to junior for more seasoning. But his demotion would last only one-quarter of the season. There was still no room between the pipes for Mike Vernon, who spent the bulk of the season in the minors.

The Flames opened up their new season on the road, posting one win, one loss and one tie in their first three games. On October 15, a full house packed the brand new Saddledome to watch the Flames renew the Battle of Alberta. After the ceremonial faceoff between Wayne Gretzky and Lanny McDonald, the two teams fought a tooth-and-nail battle for the next 60 minutes of play. In the end, it was the Oilers who came out on top with a 4–3 win.

The Flames gave as good as they got over the remainder of the season, proving they could play with any other team in the league. Badger Bob and Fletcher kept the lineup fresh by rotating young-sters in and out all season long. Dan Quinn was called up from the minors and played 54 games with the club. Enforcer Tim Hunter played in 43 contests after squeaking into only 18 games in the previous two years. Defenseman Al MacInnis stuck with the team for 51 games and made a note-worthy appearance on January 17, 1984, in a game against St. Louis. In what would be a harbinger of things to come for goalies across the league, the youngster teed up a slapshot that struck net-minder Mike Liut right in the noggin and cracked open his mask before trickling into the net.

By the end of the year, the Flames ended their two-season streak of losing records, posting a record of 34 wins, 32 losses and 14 ties for a total of 82 points. This earned them second place in the Smythe Division behind, of course, the Edmonton Oilers. Lemelin carried the bulk of the work in net. He played in 51 games, won 21, posting a 3.50 goals-against average and .893 save percentage.

The biggest surprise came on the team's forward unit as newcomer Hakan Loob proved that he deserved a place in the NHL. The Swedish forward finished the year fourth in team scoring with 30 goals and 25 assists for 55 points. Although Buffalo goaltender Tom Barrasso took home the Calder Trophy for rookie of the year, Loob was named to the all-rookie team at the end of the season.

Dan Quinn also had a standout year. Called up from the minors before Christmas, the forward got into 54 games, scoring 19 goals and 33 assists to finish fifth in team scoring. The team scoring title went once again to Kent Nils-son, who potted 31 goals and 49 assists in 67 games. Ed Beers scored 36 goals. Lanny McDon-ald played only 65 games, but he scored 33 goals and 33 assists. Doug Risebrough scored 23 goals, making him the only other player on the team to finish with more than 20 goals.

Greenhorn defensemen Jamie Macoun and Al MacInnis proved they could play well alongside the rest of the team. Called up with Paul Reinhart out of the lineup, MacInnis got into 51 games, scoring 11 goals and 34 assists. Macoun played 72 games, scoring 9 goals and helping out on 23.

The playoffs that spring looked like they'd be a repeat of the previous year, but everyone hoped the results would be different. In the opening round, Calgary ramped up the tempo on the Vancouver Canucks, sailing to 5–3 and 4–2 wins on home ice in front of packed crowds. Over-confident and assuming their victory in game three was in the bag, the Flames stumbled badly. The Canucks romped to a 7–0 win. Calgary recovered quickly from their misstep, beating Vancouver 5–1 in the fourth game to win the best-of-five series.

The Edmonton Oilers team that Calgary faced in the second round of the playoffs was a team bent on redemption. In the previous year's Stanley Cup final, the stronger, more experienced and more committed New York Islanders had overwhelmed them. This year, the Oilers were determined to take their game to the next level. They humiliated the Winnipeg Jets in the opening round, outscoring them by a combined total of 18–7. And in the second round, the Oilers were looking to keep their momentum going by beating their hated provincial rivals.

The series was everything hockey fans in the province had come to expect from the Battle of Alberta. There were highlight-reel goals, jaw-dropping saves and more than a few angry words and shoving matches. The teams split the first two games in Edmonton. The Oilers took game one 5–2. The Flames squeaked out a 6–5 win in game two. In the next two games, the Flames tripped over themselves in front of their home-town crowd, dropping game three 3–2 and game four 5–3. Standing on the cusp of playoff elimination, Calgary gave itself a collective shake and stormed onto the ice at Northlands Coliseum in Edmonton for game five. They won 5–4. Back home two nights later, the Flames repeated their triumph, scoring another 5–4 win. The stage was set for a dramatic game seven showdown to determine who would advance to the Stanley Cup semifinal. The Flames took to the Coliseum ice convinced they could outskate and outscore the up-and-coming Oilers. They made a Herculean effort. Despite their efforts, the run-and-gun Oilers were too much for the Flames, beating the Calgary team 7–4.

The Oilers went on to win their first-ever Stanley Cup against the New York Islanders, which had a lasting effect on the Flames organization. Now that their hated provincial rivals were the league champions, Calgary would have to play that much better in order to catch up.

Fortunately for the team, that summer's amateur draft would prove to be among the most fruitful in the team's history. Everyone in the NHL already knew that Mario Lemieux would be the first overall pick and that he would be going to the Pittsburgh Penguins. Picking 12th overall, the Flames settled on Ottawa 67's winger Gary Roberts, a North York boy known for his feisty, aggressive play. In 48 games during his draft year, the forward had notched 27 goals and 30 assists. He had also clocked in 144 penalty minutes.

Picking twice in the second round, Calgary first selected defenseman Ken Sabourin, then St. Louis' Paul Ranheim, who was fresh out of Edina High School in Minnesota. It would take five years for Ranheim to be ready to play with the pros. Sabourin would never fit in with the team's future plans.

Calgary's next pick came in the sixth round. Fletcher announced they were selecting British Columbia Junior Hockey League (BCJHL) winger Brett Hull. Although the BCJHL was not a hotbed of competitive hockey, Hull had left an indisputable mark on the league during his two seasons there. In his draft year, Hull scored a whopping

105 goals, coupled with 83 assists for a whopping 188 total points! (Hull came by his scoring prowess honestly—his father was Bobby Hull, an all-star with the Chicago Blackhawks in the 1960s.)

Two rounds later, Fletcher picked University of Wisconsin defenseman Gary Suter. Suter could move the puck. In 35 games, the 205-pound blueliner had racked up 51 points. But since he wasn't afraid to stand up for himself—or for his goalie or his teammates either—he had also served 110 penalty minutes.

None of the Flames' draft picks were ready for the big leagues. So, Badger Bob was going to have to work with what he had. The team had not yet had much playoff success, but it was improving. They had turned a losing record into a record that was two games above the .500 mark within only one year, which was no minor accomplishment. The task now was to improve upon that mark in the coming year.

The Flames bought into Badger Bob's team-oriented approach to the game, and he reaped the reward of their trust. The Flames won four of their first five games, outscoring their opponents 29 to 13 during that span. In four games that year, they scored nine goals against the opposing team, and in a spanking delivered to the New York Rangers, they scored 11.

The biggest test during the regular season came whenever Calgary and Edmonton faced off in the latest installments of the Battle of Alberta. These two teams played eight spirited games over the course of the schedule. Unfortunately for Calgary, the Oilers were still riding high on the wave of their Stanley Cup win from the spring before. The Flames managed only one win and one tie in the regular season series, losing the remaining six games. They could beat everyone else in the league, but not Edmonton.

Despite these losses, the team finished the season with a record that was better than it had been the year before. The Flames posted 41 wins, 27 losses and 12 ties for a total of 94 points. Kent Nilsson was again the Magic Man of the team, leading all forwards in scoring with 37 goals and 62 assists. Hakan Loob stepped up his game as well, bulging the twine 37 times and chipping in 35 assists. Back to his old self, Paul Reinhart scored 23 goals, and Ed Beers managed 28. Dan Quinn broke the 20-goal plateau for the first time as did forward Richard Kromm. The biggest surprise, however, was forward Colin Patterson. The journeyman forward had made his debut the previous year, playing in 56 games and scoring 12 times. This particular year, in 57 games, he scored 22 goals and popped in 21 assists. It was the only time in his entire career Patterson would score more than 15 goals.

Al MacInnis and Jamie Macoun were now staples on the blue line, scoring 66 and 39 points respectively. Designated goon Tim Hunter wormed his way into 71 games but spent 259 minutes in the penalty box. He also managed to chip in 22 points. That year also saw the debut of hulking 6'4" center Joel Otto, who had been signed as a free agent by the Flames after failing to be drafted. Otto played in 17 games, scoring 12 points.

Lemelin and Edwards again provided steady, reliable goaltending. Lemelin won 30 games for the first time in his career, finishing with a 3.46 goals-against average, and Edwards chipped in 11 wins in 34 games.

With their offense firing away and their young guns competing for starting jobs, the Flames felt more than ready to take on the Winnipeg Jets in the opening round of the 1985 playoffs. Of the eight regular season games the two teams had played that year, the Flames had won five, lost one and tied two. In one game, they had scored nine goals, in another, eight. Based on that record, Flames' fans felt the team should be able to handle the Jets easily. But they didn't. Living up to their Flame-out ways, Calgary dropped the series to the Jets in only four games. They managed to win a 4–0 shutout at home in game three, but dropped game one 5–4, game two 5–2 and game four 5–3.

Dejected, the Flames went home early. The Oilers won another Stanley Cup.

The finger pointing started soon after the season ended, and most of those fingers pointed squarely at the team's all-star. Kent Nilsson lived up to the wrong side of his "Magic Man" reputation. He had completely disappeared from view during the series against the Jets, even when he was on the ice. He had contributed little to the score sheet during the series, and his heart just didn't seem to be in the games.

"That was the talent I didn't have," Nilsson would later say. "Talent is stickhandling or playmaking, but you have the talent of drive, too, and maybe that was the talent I didn't have."

During the off-season, Calgary unloaded Nilsson and a conditional draft pick onto the Minnesota North Stars in exchange for a second-round pick in the 1985 and 1987 drafts. The Flames were so intent on getting rid of him, they even agreed to pay $200,000 of Nilsson's $350,000 salary for the 1985–86 season.

The money would prove to be a small sacrifice. Despite the fact that their all-time points leader was gone, the Flames would shoot to new heights without him. And one of the players they selected in the 1985 draft as a result of the deal would prove to be a more than suitable replacement.

Chapter Five

Closer than Never

By kicking their most prolific scorer off the team for failing to perform when his team needed him most, the Calgary Flames showed they were ready to start making some tough decisions about the future.

Nilsson's departure left a 100-plus-point void in the lineup that would desperately need filling if the Flames were going to contend in the upcoming season. Calgary's management had been drafting and trading to get their team the offense they needed. Now it was time to see if their planning had worked.

Recognizing his team needed another forward capable of scoring at least 40 goals in a season if they were going to make a run at the Stanley Cup, manager Cliff Fletcher focused on finding a goal scorer in the 1985 amateur draft. Although he squandered the team's first-round pick on American defenseman Chris Biotti, who would never play a game in the NHL, Trader Cliff put the second-round pick Minnesota had flipped to him in the Nilsson trade to good use. While the three teams picking before the Flames grabbed goalies, Fletcher focused on Joe Nieuwendyk, a young Ontario boy who was scoring up a storm in the National Collegiate Athletic Association (NCAA). Nieuwendyk was born in Oshawa, Ontario, and had wowed scouts with his prowess in the faceoff circle and his scoring ability. He was also an excellent lacrosse player, winning the Minto Cup in 1984 with the Whitby Warriors. But hockey was Nieuwendyk's passion, and he enrolled at Cornell University for the 1984–85 school year, scoring 21 goals and 24 assists in 29 games his first season. That performance was good enough to grab the attention of the Flames' scouting staff, who admired the 6'2" forward's sense of the play unfolding around him and his strength on the puck. Everyone believed it would be a couple of years before Nieuwendyk was ready to jump to the NHL, but Fletcher felt it was better to select him now and watch him develop. With the 27th pick of the draft, he selected Nieuwendyk as the Flames' future center.

With Nilsson gone, there was more room for Calgary's young players to showcase their talent on the forward lines. Joel Otto, a hulking center who had wormed his way into only a handful of games the previous year, stepped in to fill the void. Perry Berezan, a draft pick from the year before, also found himself patrolling the forward lines in 55 games. A few holes needed filling on the blue line, so youngster Gary Suter found himself anointed as a starting defenseman at the end of training camp. Neil Sheehy, a perennial tough guy who had seen action in only a smattering of Flames' games over the last two seasons, also found a permanent home on Calgary's backend.

Trader Cliff also freed up some room between the pipes in May when he sent backup goalie Don Edwards to the Toronto Maple Leafs in exchange for a fourth-round draft pick. The move ensured sparkplug goaltender Mike Vernon a place in the Flames' starting lineup, provided he was willing to play for it

If Nilsson's departure and other changes in the team had weakened the organization, it certainly didn't show during the first month of the 1985–86 season. On opening night, with memories of last spring still burning in their minds, the Flames lit up the Winnipeg Jets for eight goals in an 8–3 rout. Two nights later, Calgary blew the Los Angeles Kings out of the water by a score of 9–2. On October 28, the Battle of Alberta was again renewed, but the Oilers had the Flames' number, dousing them by a score of 6–4.

For the first quarter of the season, the Flames held their own in the Smythe Division. Between November 2 and November 19, the team lost only one game, winning six and tying two. As December approached, there was reason to believe that this year, the Flames would go far.

On December 14, two nights after notching their fourth win in five games by shutting out the Kings 5–0, the Flames dropped a close game to the Vancouver Canucks 4–3. Three nights later, the Flames lost 4–3 to the Pittsburgh Penguins. The Hartford Whalers edged past them the next night, again by a score of 4–3. What had started as a barely discernable dip in a winning season had suddenly become a freefall: the Flames went on to lose their next 11 games. No wins, no ties, no points toward their division seed. Almost all of the games were close, decided by only one or two goals, but they were often games that Calgary should have won. They lost to St. Louis, Chicago, Philadelphia, Minnesota and, of course, Edmonton.

In fact, Calgary lost twice to the Oilers in the span of less than a week. One of those games proved just how intense the rivalry between the two provincial rivals had become. On January 2, Flames forward Doug Risebrough dropped his gloves and went after Oilers tough-guy defenseman Marty McSorley. Back in 1986, the NHL had not yet required all players to use tie-down straps on their jerseys to prevent them from coming off in a fight. During the dust-up, McSorley's sweater slipped off and fell to the ice. When the linesmen moved in to separate the pair and escort them to the penalty box, Risebrough reached down and grabbed McSorley's sweater. Once inside the sin bin, Risebrough took his skate to the Oilers' jersey, shredding it to pieces before displaying it to a jubilant Saddledome crowd.

Although Edmonton won, Oilers' general manager Glen Sather was furious after the game. He told the media that he would send the Flames a bill for $1000 to replace the sweater Risebrough had destroyed.

Five nights later, the Whalers feasted on the Flames, spanking them 9–1 on home ice. This humiliating loss finally propelled Calgary past their losing ways and, on January 9, the team managed to squeak out a 5–4 win over Vancouver, the same team against whom their losing streak had started. By now, the Flames had dropped several places in the Smythe Division standings. If they were going to recover and qualify for the playoffs, they would have to start winning, and winning often.

But Fletcher was seeing something in his team that he didn't like. Although youngsters

Dan Quinn and Hakan Loob were moving into Nilsson's spot as the team's point producer, the Flames weren't scoring often enough to win consistently. They also lacked character and toughness, two traits that were important for any winning team. To address the most important problem—scoring—Fletcher decided to pull one of his biggest trades ever. On February 1, 1986, Trader Cliff packaged Ed Beers, Charlie Bourgeois and Gino Cavallini together and shipped them to St. Louis in exchange for Rik Wilson, Terry Johnson and American forward Joe Mullen.

Mullen's story was an interesting one. He and his brother Brian had grown up in Hell's Kitchen, New York, surrounded by drug dealers, drug addicts and prostitutes. They first learned to play roller hockey before graduating to an actual ice surface, and Mullen eventually earned an athletic scholarship to Boston College. He was later passed over in his draft year because of his diminutive 5'9" height but eventually signed a free-agent contract with the Blues. In his first year with St. Louis, Mullen scored 25 goals in 45 games, then popped in 17 markers in 49 games the next season. In 1983–84, Mullen played a full 80 games and astounded scouts everywhere, scoring 41 goals and 44 assists. He followed that up the next year with a campaign of 40 goals, 52 assists and 92 points. Now he belonged to the

Calgary Flames. At the time of the trade, Mullen had played 48 games for the Blues and had scored 28 goals.

"What a great bunch of guys," Mullen would later say about his trade to Calgary. "We had Bob Johnson as coach; he's pretty much the guy who was instrumental in getting me to Calgary in the trade. Those guys, from the first day I stepped into town, went out of their way to make me feel comfortable and be part of their organization. It was a great feeling."

Fletcher's trade for Mullen added scoring depth. Now the Flames needed a combination of leadership and tenacity to round out their roster. On March 11, Fletcher traded Rich Kromm and Steve Konroyd to the New York Islanders for John Tonelli. The forward had won four Stanley Cups in New York and was known for his clutch performances. He was a player a coach could count on to score a goal when the team needed it most. In one-on-one battles for the puck in the corners and along the boards, he was unbeatable. He was a talented faceoff man. In his best season—1981–82—Tonelli scored 35 goals and 58 assists for 93 points. When the Flames got their mitts on him, he had already scored 20.

Fletcher's trades paid huge dividends because both Mullen and Tonelli helped reverse the Flames' flagging fortunes. Of the last 10 games of the season, Calgary won six, lost three and tied one. They even thumped the Edmonton Oilers 9–4. The final sprint to the finish gave the Flames a record of 40 wins, 31 losses and 9 ties. This placed them second in the Smythe Division, 30 points behind the Oilers.

Dan Quinn picked up the bulk of the offensive slack in Nilsson's absence, scoring 30 goals and 42 assists to lead the team with 72 points. Lanny McDonald came up one point shy of Quinn's mark with 28 goals and 43 helpers of his own. Hakan Loob scored 31 in 61 games, and Jim Peplinski added 24 of his own. The biggest surprise came from Joel Otto. The tough guy lit the lamp 25 times and added 34 assists despite serving 188 penalty minutes. Sheehy and Hunter served a total of 562 penalty minutes between them. Of the new arrivals, Mullen scored 16 goals and 22 assists in the 29 games he played. Tonelli managed seven points in nine games.

On defense, the Flames discovered they had a potential superstar in draft pick Gary Suter. The American blueliner played the full 80-game season for the big club, earning 18 goals and 50 assists. These 68 points put him in a tie for third with Al MacInnis for scoring.

Meanwhile, Reggie Lemelin's play was starting to decline. Of 60 games, Calgary's veteran goaltender won only 29, losing 24 and tying 4.

His goals-against average soared to 4.08, and his save percentage fell to .872. Increasingly, Mike Vernon was forced to step in and stop pucks. Especially toward the end of the season, as Lemelin's play started to falter, Vernon increasingly relieved Lemelin during games. In 16 games, Vernon posted a record of 9 wins, 3 losses and 3 ties with a 3.61 goals-against average and a .884 save percentage. Although Vernon played only a handful of games, it became obvious that when he did, the Flames won.

For that reason, Fletcher quickly anointed Vernon as the starting goaltender for the playoffs. Stocked up on offense, with an offensively gifted blue line and a talented youngster in goal, the high-flying Flames were ready for the playoffs.

First up were the Winnipeg Jets, who had finished below Calgary in the standings. Determined not to repeat the previous year's playoff mistakes, the Flames came out of the gate at a breakneck pace. They took the play to the Jets right from the opening faceoff, winning the first game by a score of 5–1 on home ice. They followed up that victory the next night with a 6–4 triumph. Although Winnipeg kept game three close, they were unable to counter the Flames' speed and work ethic. Calgary eked out a 4–3 win to sweep the series.

The win gave the Flames a post-season date with the Oilers, a team everyone expected to make a fourth consecutive trip to the Stanley Cup finals and to bring home their third straight championship. Calgary's record against the Oilers to date gave few hopes that the Flames could pull off an upset. But Calgary planned to prove everyone wrong.

In game one, Calgary scored four goals. Mike Vernon allowed only one, giving the Flames a 1–0 series lead. Edmonton countered with a 6–5 win in game two, but the Flames rebounded to take the third game of the Smythe Division final 3–2. Two nights later, playing at the Saddledome, the Oilers slipped seven goals past Vernon. With 12 minutes left to go, Reggie Lemelin replaced the youngster, but the Oilers still won 7–4. Badger Bob gave Vernon the nod for game five, and he stepped up to the mark, surrendering only one goal in a 4–1 win that gave the Flames a 3–2 series lead heading back to the Saddledome. The Oilers staved off elimination in game six with a 5–2 win. The series was now tied at three games apiece, setting the stage for a dramatic seventh game. The winner would move on to the Campbell Conference final. The loser would have to watch the rest of the playoffs on TV.

Calgary jumped out to a lead with two quick first-period goals. The Oilers responded with a goal in the first period before tying the game on a Mark Messier goal in the second. If it wasn't decided in the next 20 minutes, game seven would be heading for overtime.

Then at the 5:19 mark of the third period, Oilers fans watched in horror as the unthinkable happened. The Flames' Perry Berezan dumped the puck into the Oilers zone and headed for the Calgary bench to change lines. Oilers defenseman Steve Smith, who was celebrating his 23rd birthday that day, corralled the puck behind the net, stopped, then attempted a breakout pass up the middle of the ice from behind the goal. The puck didn't go far. It struck the back of goaltender Grant Fuhr's skate and trickled into the Edmonton goal.

A shocked scream of anguish echoed through Northlands Coliseum as Smith collapsed to his knees. The goal was credited to Berezan because he had been the last Flame to touch the puck. The Flames led 3–2.

"I couldn't dream of it happening any better," Berezan remarked. "It's something I'll never forget. I dumped the puck in and was stepping into the bench when I heard the crowd roar. I wasn't sure what happened."

The Oilers couldn't get another puck past Mike Vernon to tie the game, so Berezan's goal—put in the net with a bit of help from Smith—was the game winner. The Flames were now one series win away from the Stanley Cup finals. As if buoyed by that knowledge, the Flames came out hard against the St. Louis Blues in the Campbell Conference final. They made up for a 3–2 loss in game one by thumping the Blues 8–2 in game two, then followed that up with a 3–2 win in game three. The Blues tied the series with a 5–2 win in game four, but Calgary took a 3–2 stranglehold lead in the series when they won 4–2 in game five. The Blues squeaked out a 6–5 win in game six to force a seventh game, but Vernon stood tall for the Flames in the deciding game, surrendering only one goal in a 2–1 win. For the first time in franchise history, the Calgary Flames were headed for the Stanley Cup finals.

The championship series would be an all-Canadian matchup between the Calgary Flames and the Montréal Canadiens—a team that had never won the Cup against a franchise that had won 23 times. The Habs trip through the post-season had been led by a quirky, Québecois rookie goaltender whose head bobbed like that of a chicken and who talked to his goal posts. His name was Patrick Roy. He would later be dubbed "St. Patrick" for his clutch goaltending work in the playoffs.

The Flames were tired. They'd played two seven-game series in a row and had only two days rest between their game seven victory against St. Louis and the first game of the Stanley Cup final in Montréal. Still, the Flames came out hard in game one, overcoming their nerves and posting a 5–2 victory. Regulation time in game two ended with the Flames and Habs tied 2–2. The game went into overtime, but on the opening faceoff, Canadiens forward Brian Skrudland pounced on the puck, swept across the Flames blue line and buried a shot past a surprised Mike Vernon. The elapsed time from faceoff to game-winning goal was nine seconds. It was the fastest game winner ever scored in Stanley Cup history.

The goal was a watershed moment for the Habs. In front of a Saddledome jubilantly celebrating the Flames' post-season success, the Canadiens pulled out a 5–3 win in game three. Two nights later, both Vernon and Roy were playing their best hockey of the playoffs—the score was 0–0 as both goaltenders turned aside their opponents' increasingly desperate efforts to score. With nine minutes left in the third period, Doug Risebrough trapped the puck in the Flames zone and sent an ill-advised clearing pass out of his own end. The Canadiens' Claude Lemieux jumped on the bad clearing attempt and fired it right past Vernon. It was the only goal of the game. When the final buzzer sounded, the two teams started eyeing one another up. They exchanged words, then pushes and then punches as a full brawl erupted on the Saddledome ice. The NHL waded in after the game, meting out $42,000 in fines to all of the players involved.

It was all the Flames had. They had expended everything to get to this point in the playoffs. There was simply nothing left in the tank when the series returned to Montréal for game five. They managed to score three times, but the Habs scored four, securing yet another Stanley Cup championship.

"That's as close as I came in six years, and that may be as close as I come for another six years. I don't want to think about next year. I've got six months to think about next year. I wanted to carry the Cup around the ice," Jim Peplinski said after the game.

Calgary returned home with the Campbell Conference Trophy, but no Stanley Cup. The NHL later voted Gary Suter rookie of the year, awarding him the Calder Trophy. But the Flames weren't looking for individual success. They were looking to be the best team in the league.

They would have to wait, though not as long as Peplinski thought.

Chapter Six

Growing Pains

Coming so close to winning the cup but coming up short had been heartbreaking. But their run to the Stanley Cup final had proven something important: the Calgary Flames could now compete with every team in the league. If they played as well as they had the previous spring, they would challenge for the Stanley Cup again very soon.

Success in the coming season would have to come from the Flames' current crop of players, since the 1986 Entry Draft proved to be a total bust for Calgary. Of their 11 picks, only three ever saw ice time at the professional level, and those three only played a combined total of 15 games. Fortunately for the Flames, the team had depth in every position, so their draft results were not much of an issue.

When the Flames opened the season against the Boston Bruins on October 9, they skated to a 5–3 win. But then the team seemed to forget everything it had learned about how to win hockey games. Over the next nine games, the Flames won only twice more: once against Buffalo and once against Edmonton. They dropped the intervening six games, losing to teams like Harford, Detroit, Québec and Winnipeg. After the first 10 games of the 1986–87 season, Calgary's record stood at 3 wins and 7 losses. Worse, one of these losses was a 6–0 blowout at the hands of the Bruins in Calgary when the two teams met up for a rematch. They dropped their next game against Minnesota 7–4, then lost again one night later to Winnipeg 6–2. In Washington on November 1 for a game against the Capitals, Calgary finally pulled out a win, taking the game 4–1. That win marked the beginning of a seven-game winning streak, which included back-to-back wins against the Edmonton Oilers. Finally, the Flames seemed to have the wind back in their sails. But then, after a 4–3 win over the Hartford Whalers, the Flames dropped three straight games. At the 20-game mark, they had squeaked out a .500 record, but this was far from what their fans were expecting.

Sensing trouble, Trader Cliff made a major move to jump-start the team. On November 12, Fletcher shipped former first-round draft pick Dan Quinn to the Pittsburgh Penguins for forward Mike Bullard. At the time of the trade, Quinn's stock appeared to be falling in Calgary. In the 16 games he played with the Flames during the 1986–87 season, he had scored only three goals.

Bullard was one of the Penguins' former first-round draft picks and had been serving as team captain since 1984. His best season had come in 1983–84 when he scored 51 goals and 41 assists. He was small, standing only 5'10", but he was agile and fast. Fletcher figured he would fit in well with the dynamic, quick-skating team he was trying to build.

As the middle of November approached, the Flames finally started playing better. Although they still lost the occasional game, they managed to win at least two or three games between defeats. Eventually, the team started stringing together four-, five- and six-game winning streaks, but even then, their play could be astoundingly inconsistent. In March, for example, the team won back-to-back games against the Oilers. Five nights later, they were humiliated by the Winnipeg Jets, who pounded 10 goals into the Flames net in a 10–1 massacre.

By the end of the season, there were more games in the winning streaks than there were in the losing streaks. Calgary stood second in the Smythe and third overall in the league with a best-ever franchise record of 46 wins, 31 losses and 3 ties. Joey Mullen lived up to the promise of his first abbreviated season in a Flames' uniform and led the team in scoring with 47 goals, 40 assists and 87 points. Of all the remaining Flames forwards, only Mullen scored more than 30 in the 1986–87 season, even though many of the others had done so before. Defenseman Al MacInnis finished second in team scoring with 20 goals and 76 points. Paul Reinhart scored only 15 goals but added 54 assists for a total of 69 points. In his 28 games with the Flames, Mike Bullard scored 28 goals and 20 assists. Joel Otto slipped to only 19 goals, Hakan Loob dropped to 18 goals, and their team leader, Lanny McDonald, managed only 14 in the 68 games he played. Rookie Gary Roberts, who joined the team with only 32 games left in the season, scored five times.

Building on his strong showing in the previous season's playoffs, goaltender Mike Vernon took over from Reggie Lemelin as the starting goaltender. In 54 games, Vernon won 30 times, a mark seldom achieved by any starting goalie in the NHL. Lemelin worked his way into 34 games of his own, often relieving Vernon when the youngster started flailing between the pipes. He managed 16 wins while posting a goals-against average of 3.25.

Now the post-season beckoned, and Calgary hoped to build on the previous year's success. They had been within reach of the Stanley Cup; this year they wanted to take home hockey's Holy Grail.

But any road to the final would have to go through Edmonton. The team braced itself for that possibility as it went into its first-round series against the Winnipeg Jets. The Jets had finished third place in the Smythe, seven points behind Calgary.

The NHL had made a major change to the play-off format for the upcoming post-season, extending the first-round series from best-of-five to best-of-seven games. Their rationale was to limit the number of first-round upsets by giving the best teams a better chance of defeating those that had finished below them in the standings.

Unfortunately, the Flames didn't seemed to show up for their first-round match-up. Perhaps they were too distracted by the possibility of facing the Oilers in the playoffs and didn't focus on the task at hand. Perhaps their third-overall finish in the regular season had simply taken too much out of them. Whatever the reason, the Jets, who had finished below Calgary in the standings, made short work of the Flames. They jumped out to a 2–0 series lead with 4–2 and 3–2 wins in the first two games. Calgary eked out a 3–2 win in game three and a 4–3 victory in game five but couldn't manage any more wins. The Jets took game four 4–3, then soared to a 6–1 win in game six.

It was a stunning turn of events. Less than one year after challenging for their first-ever Stanley Cup, less than a month after finishing with their best season on record, Calgary flamed out in the first round against a weaker opponent. Fans started joking bitterly that the "C" on the Flames jerseys actually stood for "Choke."

Under Badger Bob Johnson, the team had played some of its best hockey, but the team's disappointing finish in the playoffs gave Johnson pause. During the off-season, Badger Bob, the perennial optimist who had refused to give up on his team, resigned his position as head coach of the Flames to take a position in charge of the U.S. amateur hockey program. In his place, Calgary hired a man whose attitude was as snappish as his last name.

Terry Crisp had spent 12 years playing with the Boston Bruins, St. Louis Blues, New York Islanders and the Philadelphia Flyers. As a forward with the Flyers when the team was known across the league as the Broadstreet Bullies, he had won two Stanley Cups. In his best season—1971–72 with the Blues—Crisp scored 13 goals and 18 assists in 75 games.

Since retiring from hockey, Crisp had worked as an assistant coach with the Flyers for two years immediately after he retired, then accepted a position as head coach of the Sault Ste. Marie Greyhounds of the Ontario Hockey Association. In only one season, Crisp turned the team from a squad with a losing record of 22 wins, 45 losses and 1 tie to a winning team with a record of 47 wins, 19 losses and 2 ties. Over the next five years, Crisp led the team to five winning records.

In 1985–86, the Calgary Flames hired him as the head coach of their American Hockey League affiliate, the Moncton Golden Flames. In his first season, the team finished with a record of 34 wins, 34 losses and 12 ties. The next year, they improved to 43 wins, 31 losses and no ties. Fletcher and the Calgary ownership felt Crisp was ready for the big time and promoted him from the minors to the majors as head coach of the Flames.

At his first press conference, Crisp looked out at the gathered media and made a bold declaration: "I am not Bob Johnson."

No one expected him to be. Johnson had done well in Calgary, but his coaching efforts had not been solid enough to assemble a championship team from the available talent. Crisp was being asked to take over the squad and push it further.

Fletcher's job was to provide him with the talent and skill to make it happen, but the amateur draft again seemed to yield little in the way of future prospects. Through the first seven rounds, Fletcher called the names of a succession of players who would never see any playing time in the NHL. (The exception was his second-round pick Stephan Matteau, who would play 848 games in the big leagues, but only 78 would be for the Flames.) In the eighth round, Calgary decided to gamble on a Moose Jaw Warriors winger named Theoren Fleury as the 166th overall pick of the draft.

Standing only 5'6", Fleury wasn't given much of a chance by scouts to make it in the big leagues. They thought he was too small to stand up to the physical abuse of digging in the corners. But this young man from Oxbow, Saskatchewan, had skill that was significantly disproportionate to his size and the numbers to prove it.

In his draft year, Fleury had scored 61 goals and 68 assists for the Warriors while accumulating 110 penalty minutes. He was physical despite his stature, willing to bang bodies as hard as any forward. He was also a pest, an agitator who goaded his opponents into taking questionable penalties. He got under the skin of the opposing team with both his attitude and his scoring talent. He was unlike any other player in the league and many thought he would never make it. Although he was impressive in his first training camp, the Flames sent Fleury back to Moose Jaw for more seasoning.

Some earlier draft picks finally made the jump to the big club that year. After playing in only nine games the previous season, Joe Nieuwendyk earned a place on the Flames' starting roster in training camp. So too did Brett Hull, son of legendary Chicago Blackhawks winger Bobby Hull. The powerful winger had scored 50 goals in 67 games playing for the Moncton Golden Flames the previous year under Crisp's watchful eye.

Once again Calgary started off the season on a winning note with a 5–1 victory over the Detroit Red Wings on opening night. Once again they quickly tumbled into a funk, finishing the first 10 games with a 5–5 record. But this time, their losing ways didn't last long. After the opening three weeks of the new season, the Flames never again wrestled with their game. In a 13-game span from November 1 to December 8, Calgary posted a brilliant record of 11 wins, 2 losses and 1 tie. During the rest of the season, the Flames never lost more than three consecutive games, and they only did that twice. Highlights during the season included an 11–3 win against the Toronto Maple Leafs in January and a 10–4 victory against Buffalo in March.

Yet Fletcher was not content to let the team finish the season without making some changes. Mike Vernon was having another strong season between the pipes, but even the best starting goaltender couldn't be expected to play a full 80-game season. Reggie Lemelin had signed with Boston as a free agent in the off-season. Calgary initially hoped Doug Dadswell, a free agent signing out of Cornell, could take over as Vernon's back-up, but his record in 25 games was only one game above .500. His goals-against average stood at 4.37, a high number even in the offense-minded NHL of the 1980s. At the trade deadline, Fletcher sent Steve Bozek and Brett Hull, who had scored 26 goals and 24 assists in 52 games, to the St. Louis Blues in exchange for goaltender Rick Wamsley and defenseman Rob Ramage. Ramage was a former first-round draft pick of the Colorado Rockies. Wamsley had been a fifth-round pick of the Montréal Canadiens in 1979. In 31 games with the Blues that year, he won 13, lost 16, tied one and posted a 3.40 goals-against average.

Calgary continued to improve throughout the season. They ended the year with another franchise-best record, this time counting 48 wins, 23 losses and 9 ties. With 105 points, the Flames did well enough to place first in the Smythe Division. More impressively, for the first time in their history, the Flames finished first overall in the NHL.

Part of their success came from a re-energized forward unit who seemingly scored at will. The season was full of success stories for the Calgary team. The year before only Joe Mullen had scored more than 30 goals. But this year, four players broached the 40-goal mark. Hakan Loob finished the year with 106 points and became the first Swedish-born player in NHL history to score 50 goals. In his first full season as a Flame,

Mike Bullard finished second in team scoring, pocketing 48 goals, 55 assists and 103 points. Joe Mullen again hit the 40-goal mark, chipping in 44 assists in an 84-point campaign.

But the biggest surprise came from first-year center Joe Nieuwendyk. The former Cornell center scored 51 times, the second-most goals ever scored by a rookie in the history of the league. Mike Bossy had scored 53 in his first season with the Islanders. Wayne Gretzky had scored 51 as a first-year Oiler, but he did not officially qualify as a rookie in that year because the NHL ruled his WHA playing days counted as time spent playing professional hockey. Nieuwendyk also assisted on 41 goals for a total of 92 points.

Three other Flames—Gary Suter, Al MacInnis and, before his trade, Brett Hull—punched in at least 20 goals of their own. Gary Roberts played in 74 games and scored 28 points, but also spent 282 minutes of his year sitting in the penalty box. That number, of course, paled in comparison to Tim Hunter's 337 penalty minutes. Mike Vernon saw action in 64 games, winning a personal-best 39 games while losing only 16. He posted a tidy 3.53 goals-against average.

Ensconced as the best team in regular season play, the Flames were expected to make a respectable showing in the playoffs. Calgary faced off against the Los Angeles Kings in the opening round, a team the Flames had finished 37 points ahead of in the league. But given the Flames' record in previous post-seasons, Calgary fans were leery of labeling any series win a sure thing.

The Flames made quick work of the Kings. They stormed to a 9–2 win in game one and followed that up with a 6–4 victory two nights later. Although the Kings pulled off a 5–2 win in game three, Calgary took the series in five games with a 7–3 win in game four and a 6–4 win in game five. Since the Oilers had dusted off the Winnipeg Jets in five games in the opening round, the Flames' win set up another Battle of Alberta in the Smythe Division final.

Calgary had come out on the winning end of their regular season series with Edmonton, winning four of eight games, losing three and tying one. Given the record, everyone thought that the seven-game series would be a tight one.

It wasn't. Despite their strong season and winning record against the Oilers, Calgary couldn't manage one win against their hated provincial rivals. Edmonton took game one by a score of 3–1. Gretzky scored in overtime for a 5–4 win in game two. Things didn't improve for Calgary once they went to Edmonton. The Oilers outscored them 4–2 in game three and 6–4 in game four, sweeping the Flames from the post-season.

The Oilers went on to win the Stanley Cup against the Boston Bruins as the Flames players watched from home. One month later, at the NHL awards presentation, Joe Nieuwendyk stepped forward and accepted the Calder Trophy as the league's rookie of the year. Given his 51-goal freshman campaign, no one had doubted that he would be the player who ended up taking the hardware home.

But Nieuwendyk's win didn't take away the sting of the Flames' devastating loss in the play-offs.

"We knew once training camp started the next year that we had 25 guys who had put aside personal goals," Al MacInnis said. "Everybody was hungry. Everybody wanted the same thing. Everybody wanted to win the Stanley Cup."

The Flames spent the rest of the summer looking back on their four-game sweep by the Edmonton Oilers, wondering how they were ever going to find a way to beat a team that boasted not just the best forward in the game, but the greatest player to ever play the sport.

The solution came not in Calgary, but in Edmonton. On August 9, 1988, Oilers' owner Peter Pocklington traded Wayne Gretzky to the Los Angeles Kings.

Chapter Seven

All the Way

The biggest surprise in NHL history came that August when Peter Pocklington traded Wayne Gretzky to LA. Gretzky was the Oilers' best goal scorer. Possessed of an uncanny sixth sense that enabled him to see the ice in a completely different way from anyone else, he was also their best playmaker, making 50-goal scorers out of many of his teammates. Pocklington, however, was running into a cash crunch in Edmonton, and Gretzky wasn't getting any younger. With every year he played in the NHL, his value was bound to decline, so Pocklington decided to act. Shortly after Gretzky's wedding to actress Janet Jones, Pocklington essentially sold Wayne Gretzky to the Los Angeles Kings for millions of dollars, forward Jimmy Carson and a whole raft of draft picks.

Now Gretzky was gone. He would still be playing in the same division as the Flames in the Smythe, but he was no longer the heart and soul of the Oilers team. The playing field was finally level in the Battle of Alberta.

The draft turned out to be another disappointment for the Flames. Their first-round pick, goaltender Jason Muzatti, would go on to play only two games for the team. With little in the way of talent left by the 12th round, Fletcher again looked beyond the Iron Curtain in the Soviet Union and drafted the Russian Sergei Pryakhin, a right-winger who had played the last few seasons with the Kryjla Sovetov Russian club team. He was also the last player selected in the draft, 252nd overall.

Fletcher still wanted someone with grit, someone who played with tenacity and heart to toughen up the forward unit. So, on September 5, he pulled off another blockbuster deal, sending Mike Bullard, Craig Coxe and Tim Corkery to the St. Louis Blues for Mark Hunter, Steve Bozek, Mike Dark and embattled center Doug Gilmour.

Originally drafted in 1984 by the St. Louis Blues, Gilmour had proven himself to be a gifted scorer and faceoff man for the Blues. After three straight 20-goal seasons, Gilmour potted 42 goals in 1986–87, then 36 in 1987–88. The Blues had absolutely no intention of letting Gilmour go, but events beyond their control forced them to deal him away. A local family had filed a $1 million lawsuit against Gilmour. In the suit, the family alleged that he had repeatedly sexually abused their teenage daughter, who often babysat for his family.

Everyone seemed to agree that the lawsuit against Gilmour was without merit. Indeed, before the suit was even filed, the family had approached the Blues organization and asked for $200,000 in exchange for not going public with the allegations. The family never asked the police to investigate, and no criminal charges were ever laid. The prosecuting attorney for the city later told the media he was investigating the family on possible charges of extortion.

But despite general agreement that the accusations were false, the media would not let go of the story and hounded both Gilmour and his teammates by seeking comments. Ultimately, the situation proved to be a distraction for the team, and they had no choice but to trade Gilmour away. Gilmour was eager to be out from under the cloud of suspicion and agreed to go.

The Calgary Flames welcomed Gilmour into the fold immediately, quickly anointing him as one of their key faceoff men. Aside from the addition of "Dougie," the Flames' opening night lineup in the 1988–89 season looked little different from the one that had been beaten so mercilessly by Edmonton the previous spring.

Nieuwendyk, Mullen, McDonald, Suter, Roberts and Vernon were all back.

On October 6, the team tied the Islanders 4–4, then dropped a close 6–5 game to Los Angeles. They went on to beat Detroit 5–2, the Gretzky-less Oilers 6–1 and the Los Angeles Kings 11–4. At the 10-game mark, the team was sitting on 5 wins, 2 losses and 3 ties. Between November 10 and December 8, the Flames won 12 games and tied one, propelling them into first place both in the Smythe Division and the league. In their eight games against the Oilers, the Flames took advantage of Edmonton's struggles to learn how to play without Gretzky. The Flames lost only twice, winning five games and tying one.

During Calgary's remarkable performance in the regular season, Lanny McDonald was aiming to reach two separate milestones of his own. The long-time forward could, if the season continued, notch his 500th career goal and 1000th career point, but his chances seemed slim. He was getting old, his playing time was starting to decrease and his scoring had declined substantially over the last three seasons. Many wondered if this might be his last season in the NHL. He was still the heart and soul (and mustache) of the team, but his skills were starting to wane.

But then on March 7, 1989, McDonald scored an assist during the Flames' 9–5 barnstorming win over the Winnipeg Jets. It was his 1000th point. Now, as the season wound down, everyone began to wonder if he would score his 500th goal as well.

When McDonald suited up for the March 21 game against the New York Islanders, he had 499 career goals. One more would put him at 500. Late in the game, McDonald grabbed the puck behind the Islanders net, stepped out and scored on a classic wrap-around play. The Saddledome roared as McDonald pumped his fists in the air. Now there was only one challenge left for Lanny McDonald to surmount—winning the Stanley Cup.

The Flames were having an excellent regular season but still needed more grit on the team. To that end, they reached down into their farm team, now in Salt Lake City, Utah, and called up Theoren Fleury, who was having an outstanding season at the minor pro level. In 40 games, Fleury had scored 37 goals and 37 assists.

But the Flames weren't just calling him up for his scoring ability. They needed his gritty approach to the game. In December 1987, his draft year, Theoren Fleury had been selected by Team Canada to represent the country at the annual World Junior Hockey Championship. The tournament was played in Piestany, Czechoslovakia, which at the time was still a member of the Soviet-dominated Warsaw Pact.

During a game between the Soviets and Canada, Fleury ended up squaring off against Pavel Kostichkin in a fight in the second period. The fight quickly snowballed into a bench-clearing brawl. The referee and linesmen fled from the ice. It took 20 minutes for tournament organizers to restore order and then only by turning off the lights in the rink. After the "Punch-up at Piestany" concluded, organizers expelled both the Soviet and Canadian teams from the tournament. Fleury returned to the junior team in 1988, where he won a gold medal.

Once he started playing with the Flames, Fleury performed surprisingly well. He scored almost one point per game in 36 games, finishing the year with 14 goals and 20 assists.

Days before the team's March 31, 1989 game against the Winnipeg Jets, Trader Cliff announced a new surprise. He had successfully negotiated the release of Sergei Pryakhin from the USSR, and the Soviet forward would play his first game against the Jets. The entire hockey world was tickled by the idea. Never before had a member of the Soviet national hockey team been allowed by his government to move to North America and play professional hockey in the NHL. The media weren't sure what to expect, wondering if Pryakhin would be an agile, deft puckhandler who could skate his way through any team, or a physically soft player unaccustomed to the speed and body-banging style of North American play.

The fanfare preceding Pryakhin's debut was more noteworthy than his play. The Russian played in the Flames' last two games of the year against the Jets and the Oilers. The team won both, but Pryakhin didn't record a single point in either contest.

It was another successful season for Calgary. They finished first overall in the league, a few points ahead of the Montréal Canadiens. Building on their string of better-than-ever seasons, the Flames set another franchise record with 54 wins, 17 losses and 9 ties. They had 117 points for the season and finished first in the Smythe, in the Campbell Conference and in the league.

Joe Mullen had his best season to date, finishing first in scoring for the Calgary Flames with 51 goals, 59 assists and 110 points. The newcomer Doug Gilmour proved himself an important addition to the team, scoring 26 goals with 59 assists to tie Hakan Loob for second in team scoring with 85 points. Joe Nieuwendyk shook off the threat of a "sophomore jinx" by firing home another 51 goals. In a January 11 game versus the Winnipeg Jets, the youngster scored five times in one game.

Defensemen Gary Suter and Al MacInnis each continued to play strong, finishing the year with 58 and 49 points respectively. Joel Otto fired home 20 goals of his own, while second-year player Gary Roberts passed the 20-goal mark for the first time, potting 22. Tim Hunter set a new team record for penalty minutes with 375. Lanny McDonald's play continued to decline: he scored only 11 goals and 7 assists in 51 games. For the first time in his career, McDonald found himself watching games from the press box, scratched from the lineup in favor of another player.

The Flames could score, their defense was sound and their goaltenders were playing some of their best hockey ever. For the first time in his career, Mike Vernon posted a goals-against average below 3.00, surrendering a mere 2.65 goals per game while winning 37 of 52 contests. Rick Wamsley proved he was as capable as any backup in the league, winning 17 of 35 starts and posting a 2.96 goals-against average. Only the Montréal Canadiens tandem of Patrick Roy and Brian Hayward surrendered fewer goals.

Calgary's first-place finish secured the team home-ice advantage for the playoffs for the duration of the post-season. Their first round opponents turned out to be the Vancouver Canucks, a fast, hard-working team led by the strong play of goaltender Kirk MacLean. (MacLean, Vernon and Roy would all be finalists for the league's Vezina Trophy for best goaltender that year.) The series was tough and hard fought as the teams traded wins back and forth. In game one, Paul Reinhart, a former Flame and one of the better players to leave the team, scored the game winner early in overtime, giving the Canucks a 4–3 win. Calgary responded two nights later with a 5–2 triumph. Vernon held down the fort in game three, posting a 4–0 shutout that gave the Flames a 2–1 series lead. Vancouver battled back in game four with a 5–3 win before running into Vernon again on a night when he couldn't be beaten. Calgary took a 3–2 series lead with the 4–0 game-five win, but couldn't put the series away in Vancouver, losing 6–3 in game six. Two nights later, the teams returned to Calgary for game seven.

This final game of the Smythe Division semi-final turned into one of the most exciting hockey matches in recent memory. For Calgary Flames fans, it was also one of the most agonizing. Both MacLean and Vernon played brilliantly, making dazzling saves. At the end of regulation time, the score was tied 3–3, and game seven headed into overtime. The first goal would win the series.

Early in overtime, Vancouver forward Stan Smyl caught the Calgary defense napping, grabbed a pass along the right wing boards and scampered in unmolested from the blue line. He threw a head fake at Vernon, then snapped the puck high to Vernon's glove hand. Unfazed by Smyl's attempt to deke him, Vernon kicked out his left leg, flashed the leather of his catcher and pulled a sure goal out of the air.

Minutes later, the Flames rushed up ice into the Vancouver zone. Jim Peplinski crossed the Vancouver blue line in transition and did what any good hockey player without a solid scoring chance would do—he just threw the puck on net and prayed something would happen. Something did. The puck caromed off Joel Otto's skate; he was tangling with a Vancouver defenseman in front of MacLean and slipped past the helpless goaltender. The Saddledome erupted in jubilation and relief as the Flames took the first round by a score of 4–3.

The Oilers had made it to the playoffs in their first year without Gretzky but had then fallen victim to their own trade. The Great One was still part of the Smythe Division, and in the first round, he led his new-look Kings to victory over his ex-teammates. That meant that, although the Flames didn't have to face Edmonton, they still had to face Gretzky.

Wayne's Kings, however, were not Wayne's Oilers. Only the first game—a 4–3 win by the Flames over the Kings on home ice—was close. Two nights later, the Flames pounded eight pucks past Kings goalie Kelly Hrudey for an 8–3 win. Calgary finished the sweep in Los Angeles, beating the Kings 5–2 in game three and 5–3 in game four.

The series win set up a Campbell Conference final between Calgary and the Chicago Blackhawks. The Blackhawks lineup was deep, featuring 40-goal scorer Steve Larmer, dazzling skater and puckhandler Denis Savard, veteran Dirk Graham and rugged defenseman Dave Manson. A 24-year-old forward named Greg Gilbert had also worked his way into the Hawks lineup during the regular season.

Chicago might have been good, but in this series, Calgary was better. Vernon got his third shutout of the post-season as the Flames blanked the Blackhawks 3–0 in game one. Chicago countered with a 4–2 win in game two, but it was all they could muster. Calgary went on to win the series in five, winning the remaining three games of the series by scores of 5–2, 2–1 and 3–1. Three years after their first appearance in the Stanley Cup final, the Calgary Flames were ready once again to play for professional hockey's most coveted prize.

Their opponents were again the Montréal Canadiens. During the playoffs, the Canadiens had swept the Hartford Whalers in four straight games, trounced the Boston Bruins in five and beaten the Philadelphia Flyers in six games. The final was the kind of match-up the league relished: the two top teams during the regular season battling it out for the league championship. There was no underdog in this series.

The series opened up in Calgary on May 14. The first four goals were all scored in the first 10 minutes of the game. Stéphane Richer beat Vernon on a power play to open the scoring, but Al MacInnis responded with two goals of his own to give Calgary a 2–1 lead. Larry Robinson tied the game shortly afterwards. Theoren Fleury scored the game winner in the second period, giving game one to the Flames with a score of 3–2.

Montréal came out flying two nights later, jumping to a 2–0 lead by the two-minute mark of the second period. Goals by Nieuwendyk and Otto tied the game later in the second, but the Canadiens scored twice more in the third, tying the series at one. Back in Montréal for game three, the teams finished regulation time tied at 3–3. With Flames forward Mark Hunter's overtime penalty set to expire with just under two minutes left to play in the first overtime, Canadiens forward Ryan Walter banged home the game winner to give Montréal a 4–3 win and a 2–1 series lead.

Calgary took the two days between games three and four to regroup and came out firing in the first period of game four, directing 13 shots at Patrick Roy, all of which he turned away. In the second period, both Doug Gilmour and Joey Mullen scored to put the Flames up 2–0. The Canadiens scored, narrowing the gap, but Al MacInnis scored too, increasing the Flames' lead to two. Claude Lemieux scored one more for the Canadiens, but they couldn't beat Vernon to tie the game, and Calgary added an empty-netter to seal the win. The series was now tied 2–2.

In front of his home crowd, and only 28 seconds into game five, Joel Otto scored, and the Flames never looked back. When the first period was over, the Flames were up 3–1. Mike Vernon continued to stand on his head, allowing only one more goal, a second-period shot by Mike Keane. The 3–2 victory gave the Flames a 3–2 series lead heading back to Montréal. One more win and they would finally realize their goal of being the Stanley Cup champions. But history was against them: no team had ever won the Stanley Cup on the ice of the Montréal Forum except for the Montréal Canadiens.

Then there was the problem of McDonald. The heart and soul of the Flames for the last nine years, his team was now on the cusp of winning the Stanley Cup, but he had yet to see a minute of ice time in the finals. As game six approached, McDonald wondered if he would ever get to play in a Flames' uniform again.

But head coach Terry Crisp was not without class. With game six approaching and his team poised to win its first-ever championship, Crisp dressed McDonald and sat out Tim Hunter and Jim Peplinski.

Wearing the captain's C, McDonald stepped out onto the ice of the Montréal Forum for the last time. Almost 15 years before as a Toronto Maple Leaf, McDonald had scored his first-ever NHL goal here. It brought things full-circle to play what might be his final game on the same sheet of ice.

The atmosphere was tense. Flames forward Colin Patterson scored the only goal of the first period, but Claude Lemieux erased the Flames lead early in the second period. Three minutes later, Joe Nieuwendyk started a rush up-ice just as a minor penalty to McDonald expired. As the pair crossed the line, Nieuwendyk fired a shot on net that Roy kicked aside. The rebound went straight to Lanny McDonald, who gobbled it up and cracked it into the net to give the Flames a 2–1 lead. McDonald rounded the Canadiens net with a look of sheer joy on his face, pumping both hands in the air. He had just scored the last goal of his career, and the timing couldn't have been better.

Halfway through the third period, Doug Gilmour scored to put Calgary up 3–1. Rick Green scored less than a minute later, reducing the lead to one goal. With the clock winding down, the Canadiens pulled Roy in favor of an extra attacker.

With just over a minute to go, Gilmour slipped the puck into the empty net to increase the Flames' lead to two goals. The remaining 63 seconds felt like an eternity for the Calgary team as they waited for the buzzer to sound. When it did, the team erupted from the bench to swarm their goaltender. Peplinski and Hunter, clad only in their one-piece Flames red underwear, came flying out of the dressing room to join the celebration. After 17 years as a franchise and nine years in Calgary, the Flames had finally won the Stanley Cup.

Most of the Montréal fans hung around to watch as NHL president John Ziegler awarded the Conn Smythe Trophy to Al MacInnis as the most valuable player in the playoffs that year. The defenseman had led the team in scoring with 7 goals and 24 assists for 31 points.

Then, in a moment that couldn't have been scripted better by Hollywood, Ziegler handed the Stanley Cup to Flames captain Lanny McDonald.

Coach Crisp later attributed the Flames commitment to victory to their abbreviated playoff run the year before.

"The biggest thing was being swept four straight by Edmonton the year before," said Crisp. "We spent a long summer looking at what we did wrong. We came to the conclusion we didn't play patient defense. The Canadiens played tight, tough defensive hockey, and we were able to match that. That was the difference."

The Flames knew about the Forum's history coming in but they didn't seem to care.

"The mystique of the Forum didn't phase us," said MacInnis.

For his part, McDonald had little to say. Later that night, as the Flames celebrated in their dressing room, someone snapped a photo of him, clad only in his long johns, sporting a Flames' "Stanley Cup Champions" hat, cradling the Cup close to his face as he might a child. His playoff beard rivaled the size of his mustache, and his eyes were closed, as if he was drinking in every last ounce the moment had to offer.

After the Flames returned to Calgary, McDonald confirmed what everyone expected. The player who had helped build the Stanley Cup–winning team from the moment he arrived in the city planned to retire.

Surprisingly, he wasn't the only one.

Chapter Eight

The Long Way Down

Lanny McDonald's retirement after the Calgary Flames' Stanley Cup win in the 1989 season came as no surprise to anyone. The Flames' captain was 36 years old. He'd been playing professional hockey since the early 1970s and was due for some time off.

"I was part of the on-ice lineup for that winning game, and we were the only team, other than the Canadiens, to ever win the Stanley Cup on Forum ice. All those things added up to me thinking, 'Boy, it's a sign. It's time I was out of here.' What a great way to go," McDonald reflected.

Hakan Loob's departure caught everyone by surprise. During the off-season, he announced to the Flames that he would not return for another season. Loob had been a scoring powerhouse for the Flames since his rookie year, was the first Swedish-born forward ever to score 50 goals in a season in the NHL and had been an integral part of the Stanley Cup–winning team. But now he wanted to go back to Sweden to raise his family, and the Flames couldn't change his mind. His presence in the locker room would be missed— his points on the score sheet even more so.

Once again the draft produced few picks with any potential. The best player the Flames called during the annual event was Robert Reichel, a Czech center who had scored 23 goals and 25 assists in 44 games for Litvinov Chemopetrol. The remainder of Calgary's picks played a combined total of 40 games for the club. But Fletcher wasn't that worried. One of his moves the previous season was starting to pay off big time, not just for the Flames but for the NHL as a whole.

The Flames had showcased for the first time ever the skills of a Soviet hockey player when Sergei Pryakhin played for the team in two games the previous year. Fletcher's negotiations to secure Pryakhin's playing rights had weakened the iron grip the USSR kept on its best hockey players. In the 1989–90 season, other Soviets started trickling into the league, making the hop over the Atlantic Ocean to join the clubs that had drafted them. Few had ever been exposed to life outside of the Iron Curtain and fewer still spoke a word of English.

One of the players who made the jump that season was Sergei Makarov. Drafted by the Flames in the 12th round of the 1983 NHL draft, the right-winger was only 18 months removed from winning the gold medal with the USSR national team at the 1988 Winter Olympics in Calgary. When he arrived in Calgary, he was 31 years old and required no further time in the minors to bring his game up to speed. Unfortunately for the Flames, Makarov arrived without Igor Larionov and Vladimir Krutov, the two line-mates with whom Makarov had played on the feared KLM line. The Vancouver Canucks had drafted both Larionov and Krutov and were hanging on to both.

As a part of the thawing relations between East and West, the Calgary Flames spent their pre-season touring the Warsaw Pact countries, playing exhibition games in the Soviet Union and Czechoslovakia. When they returned to Canada, the roster was pretty much set. Theoren Fleury had earned himself a permanent spot on the roster as had Makarov. The Flames won their first three games of the year and seemed ready to cruise to another first-place finish in the league.

But six games into the year, the team sustained a blow it hadn't seen coming. Jim Peplinski, who had been playing with the team since they had first arrived in Calgary, announced that he was retiring. He said the game just wasn't fun anymore, which was odd for a 29-year-old to say, but there was nothing Calgary could do to stop him. Peplinski eventually started up a car dealership branded with his name.

With the departures of McDonald, Loob and Peplinski, the team lost three of its veteran players and its proven leaders. McDonald and Peplinski had shared the captaincy. The team named Brad McCrimmon, a defenseman who had been playing in the background in Calgary since 1987, to replace them.

After Peplinski left the team, there were few surprises for the rest of the season. Makarov proved to be as good in the NHL as he had been at the international level, scoring 24 goals and 62 assists for 86 points. He finished fourth in team scoring. Joe Nieuwendyk was first with 45 goals and 50 assists for 95 points. Doug Gilmour was second with 24 goals and 67 assistant for 91 points. Al MacInnis was third with 28 goals and 62 assists for 90 points. Joe Mullen played in all but two games but scored only 36 times. Theoren Fleury continued to impress, scoring 31 goals and 35 assists in his first full season. Vernon and Wamsley continued to provide solid goaltending, winning 23 and 18 games respectively.

By the end of the year, the defending Stanley Cup champs had faltered slightly, failing to match their performance from the previous season. They finished first in the Smythe but second in the NHL with a record of 42 wins, 23 losses and 15 ties. The Los Angeles Kings were scheduled to play the Flames in the first round of the playoffs. Since the Flames had swept the Kings the previous year, everyone thought this would be a decisive Calgary win, but they were wrong.

The Kings were led by Wayne Gretzky, who had found his stride in LA and was again making everyone who played with him better. The Kings upset the Flames, humiliating them in a 12–4 blowout in game four on the Kings' home ice before going on to win the series in six games.

Few coaches can survive having their team go from league champion to first-round loser in the course of one season. Even though he had won Calgary its first-ever Stanley Cup, Terry Crisp was fired by the Flames during the off-season. Fletcher tapped former Flames player Doug Risebrough to succeed Crisp as coach.

Sergei Makarov's impressive rookie season left the NHL in a quandary. Without a doubt, the Soviet winger had been the best of all the first-year players in the NHL that season, but he was also 31 years old, well beyond the age at which most players first start playing professionally. There was no rule in the NHL book stating that a rookie had to be young to win the Calder Trophy for rookie of the year, but the league was still hesitant to bestow the honor on someone so old.

In the end, Makarov's play spoke for itself, and the league awarded him the trophy. *The Hockey News* best described the conflict in a cartoon that depicted Makarov, clad in full hockey gear, holding the trophy in both hands and shouting at the crowd, "No, the rookie of the year's father is not here accepting the trophy on his behalf!" Starting the following season, the NHL amended its rules for rookies, declaring only players 27 years of age and under could qualify for the Calder.

Fletcher hung on to the core of his team for the 1991–92 season, thinking the Flames still had the talent to challenge for the Cup. He used the team's first-round pick in the draft to select goaltender Trevor Kidd of the Brandon Wheat Kings, picking him over a young St. Hyacinthe Lasers puckstopper named Martin Brodeur. Fletcher also traded perennial 40-goal-scorer Joey Mullen to Pittsburgh for fear Mullen was getting too old to play consistently. In return, the Flames received defenseman Nicolas Perreault. Mullen would go on to win two Stanley Cups with the Penguins. Perreault never made it to the big leagues.

The team's record held steady at 46 wins, 26 losses and 8 ties, locking up second place in the Smythe

Division and fourth in the league. Theoren Fleury led the team in scoring, becoming quite possibly the shortest player ever to score 50 goals. Nieuwendyk scored 45, Makarov 30 and Roberts 22. Robert Reichel, a draft pick from 1989, debuted with the team, scoring 19 goals and 41 points in 66 games.

Again the Flames went into the playoffs ranked near the top of the league. And again they failed to escape the first round. The Gretzky-less Oilers knocked them out in a hard-fought seven-game series.

It was obvious the team needed change, but when it came, it came as a shock. At the end of the season, "Trader Cliff" Fletcher announced he was leaving to become president and general manager of one of the NHL's most storied franchises: the Toronto Maple Leafs. After 19 years, the man who had built the team from its early days in Atlanta into a competitive Canadian team was now leaving the organization. It was a sad departure but a necessary one. After Fletcher left, the Flames ownership appointed Risebrough general manager. With Fletcher gone, the Flames sagged.

The team got another nasty shock on November 26, when former coach "Badger Bob" Johnson died of brain cancer. Johnson had been coaching the Pittsburgh Penguins and had led them to the

Stanley Cup the previous spring. His death was felt across the hockey world, but many of the Flames players had played for him, and it hit them especially hard.

Weeks later, Doug Gilmour delivered yet another body blow to the team. Player salaries were rising across the league, and in a market like Calgary, where the Canadian dollar was valued at only three-quarters the American dollar and the overall hockey market was much smaller, the Flames were having problems keeping up. Gilmour felt he deserved a new contract, and on January 1, 1992, informed Risebrough that he would not play for the team again.

One day later, Risebrough responded to Gilmour's walkout by making what most Flames fans still view today as "the worst trade in history." Risebrough decided to swing a deal with former boss Cliff Fletcher, who had always liked the player. Risebrough packaged together Doug Gilmour, Rick Wamsley, Kent Manderville and Jamie Macoun and shipped them to the Maple Leafs in exchange for Gary Leeman, Michel Petit, Alexander Godynuck and goaltender Jeff Reese.

Three months later, the Vancouver Canucks annihilated the Flames 11–0 in what was one of the Flames' worst efforts in recent memory. Risebrough resigned as coach the next day, choosing instead to focus on his general managing duties.

Guy Charron, a former Red Wings player who had been working as an assistant coach for the Flames since 1990, was appointed in his place. The move had little effect on the team, who earned 2 wins, 5 losses and 1 tie during Chadron's 19-day tenure. On March 22, Dave King, the coach who had turned Canada's Olympic hockey program into a model of amateur development worldwide, took over behind the bench.

Joe Nieuwendyk took over as captain, and Gary Roberts assumed the team-scoring lead with 53 goals, passing the 50-mark for the first time in his career. Fleury added 33 goals of his own. Hampered by injuries, Makarov and Nieuwendyk only managed 22 goals apiece. Of the three skaters received in the Doug Gilmour trade, Michel Petit scored the most points, accumulating 3 goals and 10 assists in 36 games with the team. Gilmour scored 49 points for Toronto in 40 games. At season's end, the Flames had posted a losing record of 31 wins, 37 losses and 12 ties. For the first time since their arrival in Calgary from Atlanta, the Flames missed the playoffs.

Under King's coaching scheme, Calgary improved significantly the following season. Robert Reichel put 40 goals in the net and racked up 28 assists. Theoren Fleury finished first in team scoring, lighting the lamp 34 times and adding 66 assists for 100 points. Gary Roberts and Joe Nieuwendyk scored 38 times, Sergei Makarov only 18 times and Joel Otto 19 times. The team finished with a record of 43 wins, 30 losses and 11 ties. They were second in the Smythe Division and ninth overall in the NHL. Their return to the post-season was spirited but brief as Gretzky and the Kings again knocked the Flames out of the playoffs, winning the opening round series in six games.

Reichel, Roberts, Fleury and MacInnis all returned to the team for the 1993–94 season, and they all continued to put points on the board. Roberts scored 41 goals, and Reichel and Fleury each scored 40, while MacInnis added 54 assists. King also promoted Trevor Kidd, the team's "goalie of the future" to back up Mike Vernon.

Risebrough, however, started making trades with his players. On March 11, 1994, he put together a six-player deal with the Hartford Whalers, sending Gary Suter, Paul Ranheim and Ted Drury south for Zarley Zalapski, James Patrick and Michael Nylander. It was the second major shake up in the team's roster in three years, but this time the effect was more positive. Unlike the four players who had come over in the Gilmour trade, these players settled into the team quickly and started contributing right away. In 10 games, Zalapski, a puck-moving defenseman, contributed 10 points.

The team's record improved marginally to 42 wins, 29 losses and 13 ties, which was good enough for first place in the newly named Pacific Division. But regular season success did not translate into post-season victories. The Flames ran headlong into a hot Vancouver Canucks team that opened the series with a 5–0 shutout of the Flames. Calgary managed to drag the series to seven games but bowed out of the playoffs after the first round.

Fans across North America were forced to wait an extra 103 days for the 1994–95 season to begin as both players and owners squared off in a lockout over their failure to negotiate a new collective bargaining agreement. By the time the lockout ended, there was only enough time to salvage a 48-game schedule.

The threat of the lockout hadn't stopped Risebrough from making significant changes to the team. During the off-season, he parted with long-time Flames goaltender Mike Vernon, sending him to Detroit for defenseman Steve Chiasson. The big trades didn't stop there. One month after Vernon left, Risebrough was forced into trading one of his team's most consistent players. Defensive icon Al MacInnis was scheduled to become a restricted free agent, and the Flames

would not be able to match the offers he received
from other teams. So Risebrough traded him to
the St. Louis Blues for Phil Housley and a pair of
second-round draft picks. Housley was known as
a puck-moving defenseman and quickly proved
that he could take most of the slack left behind
by MacInnis' departure. In the 43 games of the
abbreviated 1994–95 season, he scored 8 goals
and 35 assists.

Fleury played in all but one of the 48 games,
leading the team with 29 goals and 29 assists.
Nieuwendyk popped in 21, and Reichel followed
up with 18 goals of his own. Trevor Kidd proved
that he was ready to take over from Vernon,
winning 22 of 43 starts and posting a respectable 2.61 goals-against average. Kidd, however,
wasn't ready for the playoffs, and neither was
the rest of the team. Despite a record of 24 wins,
17 losses and 7 ties that secured them first place
in the Pacific Division, the Flames couldn't get
out of the first round of the post-season. Up three
games to two in the first round of the playoffs
against the San Jose Sharks and needing only
one win to clinch the series, the Flames stumbled badly, dropping both game six and game
seven.

The third-straight first-round loss inevitably
cost King his job as coach. He had made the team
better during the regular season, but couldn't

seem to win in the post-season. Risebrough tapped former Calgary assistant coach and Québec Nordiques head coach Pierre Page to take over behind the bench.

Page, however, would be missing one of the Flames most potent offensive weapons. Gary Roberts had played only eight games the season before because of a degenerative condition in the discs in his neck. He elected to undergo surgery instead of continuing to play through the pain. He missed the first half of the 1995–96 season as a result. The Flames sorely missed him, especially after December when Risebrough was forced once again to part with another one of his star players.

In the changed NHL, players followed the money instead of their own sense of honor, and Nieuwendyk was proving to be too valuable for the Flames to keep. There was no way the team could afford to sign him again, and they didn't want to risk losing him on the open market when his contract expired. So Risebrough shipped him south to Dallas for Corey Millen and a young unknown prospect—Jarome Iginla.

Roberts returned to the lineup in January, posting 42 points in 35 games. Fleury led the team in scoring with 46 goals and 50 assists. Between the posts, Trevor Kidd split playing time with newcomer Rick Tabaracci. The pair won only 34 games between them and earned modest 2.78 and 2.94 goals-against averages respectively.

The Flames' record of 34 wins, 37 losses and 11 ties was barely enough to qualify for the playoffs. In the end, they might have been better off not bothering. The Chicago Blackhawks were their opponents, and the Flames never had a chance. The only benefit the 1996 post-season offered was a chance to see Jarome Iginla on the ice. He scored a goal and an assist in the two games he played. The Blackhawks took the first-round series in four straight games, holding Calgary to seven total goals while scoring 16 of their own.

The series was the last time the Calgary Flames would qualify for the playoffs for a long time. The team now looked nothing like the Calgary Flames squad that had won the Stanley Cup six years before against the Montréal Canadiens. Only Theoren Fleury and Gary Roberts remained with the team. But then at the end of the 1996 season, citing ongoing problems with his neck, Gary Roberts announced that he was retiring from the NHL.

Chapter Nine

The Years in Between

With Gary Roberts gone, Theoren Fleury was the only player left on the active roster who had been a part of the Stanley Cup–winning team of 1989. The rest of the team was a hodge-podge of middle-of-the-road players with average skills or aging players wanting to go a few more seasons before hanging up their skates.

The team's hopes rested on the one player everyone expected to mature into an elite NHL player: Jarome Iginla. Acquired the season before when the team traded away Joe Nieuwendyk, Iginla had played his way out of his hometown, St. Albert, Alberta, and into the junior hockey level, where he evolved into a talented forward who could score and hit. The Dallas Stars had drafted him with their first pick in the 1995 draft but had willingly parted with him to get their hands on Nieuwendyk. Now the winger was the Flames' property, and his performance in the two playoff games he played the season before told Page the youngster was ready for his first NHL season.

Page was operating with a new boss. Al Coates had been working with the Flames in a management position since the team had moved to Calgary from Atlanta. He replaced Risebrough as general manager, finding himself working with a team that had tons of heart but little in the way of elite NHL talent. It was a problem faced by other NHL teams in Canada. The big American teams could afford to pay the big stars big bucks, and any player who could score 20 goals could command an annual salary that was out of reach for teams like Calgary. Small-market teams like Edmonton and Calgary didn't have much in the way of revenue to draw on, so they could no longer attract star players. The Québec Nordiques and Winnipeg Jets had packed up and moved their franchises to other cities because of the economic situation. Also, there was a serious dilution of talent in the league thanks to the expansion of the early 1990s.

Coates and Page's team was only average. Theoren Fleury could qualify as a superstar, but he was the only player on the roster that could. And even he was having problems. In 1996, the forward was diagnosed with Crohn's disease, an inflammatory condition of the gastrointestinal tract. He was also struggling with a substance abuse problem. Robert Reichel's play was also starting to tail off.

Sandy McCarthy was the team's designated tough guy, and Trevor Kidd the starting goalie. The Flames picked up Dave Gagner, a former 40-goal scorer for the Minnesota North Stars who was now 33 years old, in a trade from Toronto. The rest of the team was a veritable raft of unknowns. Few people knew who Todd Hlushko, Tommy Albelin, Aaron Gavey, Glen Feather-stone and Hnat Domenichelli were, and they would never get the chance to find out. There was too little consistency in the team's roster.

The Flames finished the 1996–97 season with another losing record: 32 wins, 41 losses and 9 ties. Unlike the previous season, where they had slipped but managed to make the playoffs, this year's point total just wasn't good enough. The team's biggest problem was offense. Their opponents shut them out six times and held them to only one goal in 17 games. The Oilers, who had slipped from Stanley Cup champions to NHL bottom-dwellers, pasted Calgary 10–1 in a November 26 game. Calgary scored only 214 goals the entire season, well shy of the near-400 they had scored only a half-dozen seasons before.

The individual stats of the Flames' roster laid the problem bare. Theoren Fleury led the team in scoring with only 29 goals and 38 assists.

Suprisingly, Dave Gagner scored 27 goals, but this would be his only season with the team. German Titov scored 22 times. No one on the team scored more than 30 goals or amassed 70 points. Trevor Kidd won 21 of 55 starts, posting a 2.84 goals-against average.

Jarome Iginla was the bright spot in the sad tale of the Flames' 1996–97 season. The winger scored 21 times and added 29 assists for 50 points, leading all rookies that year in scoring. But the Calder Trophy for rookie of the year ended up going to New York Islanders defenseman Bryan Berard.

Coates quickly started making changes to the team from the top down. Brian Sutter replaced Pierre Page behind the bench on July 3, 1997. The oldest of the Sutter brothers, Brian had scored 636 points in 779 NHL games with the St. Louis Blues, then coached the team for three years. He moved on to coach the Boston Bruins for another three years before landing in Calgary.

Coates next traded starting netminder Trevor Kidd away, pairing him with Gary Roberts, who had decided to come out of retirement, to the Carolina Hurricanes in exchange for a young goalie named Jean-Sebastien Giguère and center Andrew Cassels. Halfway through the 1997–98 season, Coates shipped Zarley Zalapski and Jonas Hoglund to Montréal for Valeri Bure, the younger brother of superstar forward Pavel Bure, as well as a fourth-round draft pick. At the trade deadline, the Flames also shipped Sandy McCarthy to the Tampa Bay Lightning with a pair of draft picks in exchange for Jason Wiemer.

None of the trades did anything to salvage the possibility of a respectable finish in the 1997–98 season. The team fell even further behind than they had the previous season, finishing with only 26 wins, recording 41 losses and salvaging 15 ties. Fleury again led the team in scoring, but with only 27 goals, 51 assists and 78 points. Cory Stillman also scored 27 goals, but he only chipped in 22 assists. No other Flame managed to break the 20-goal mark. Valeri Bure scored nine points in his 16 games with the team, while Weimer counted 4 goals and 1 assist in 12. Derek Morris, a 1996 draft pick, did debut with the team and chipped in a respectable 9 goals and 20 assists. With Kidd gone, Dwayne Roloson and Rick Tabaracci split the goaltending duties, but managed only 11 and 13 wins respectively.

The 1998–99 season that followed brought Theoron Fleury great success and great disappointment. Early in the season, the Flames standout scored the 823rd point of his career to become the team's all-time scoring leader. The sparkplug seemed to have found his stride, scoring 30 goals and 39 assists in only 60 games with the team. But the Flames couldn't handle his success. Fleury was now a bona fide superstar in the last year of his contract, and Coates knew there was no way the Flames could pay him enough to make him sign a contract and stay in Calgary. So on February 28, 1999, Coates sent Fleury and winger Chris Dingman to the Colorado Avalanche for defenseman Wade Belak, prospect defenseman Robyn Regehr and leftwinger Rene Corbet. With Fleury gone, there was not a single player left on the team from the 1989 Stanley Cup–winning roster.

"I guess when you first come out of juniors, you just want to be a solid NHL player. And for me, I had the opportunity to play with some really great players along the way that have helped me," Fleury later said of his time in Calgary.

Valeri Bure and Jarome Iginla each stepped up in Fleury's absence, scoring 26 and 28 goals respectively. Cory Stillman scored 27 goals as well, but no one else on the team scored more than 12 that season. Jason Wiemer scored 8 goals, Andrew Cassels 12 and, in 20 games, Rene Corbet scored 5.

The team added two ex-Oilers to its roster: former Edmonton defenseman Steve Smith, who had sent Calgary to the Stanley Cup finals in 1986, and goaltender Fred Brathwaite. The Flames also debuted two young players who would later go on to be superstars on other teams: a young center named Martin St. Louis and a goaltender named Jean-Sebastien Giguère.

Giguère and Brathwaite were two of six contestants who took turns in the revolving door that was the Calgary Flames goal. Giguère played in net 15 times, winning four, and Brathwaite played in 28 games, recording wins in just 11. Former Leafs and Penguins backstop Ken Wregget wormed his way into 27 games but could only win 10. Youngsters Tyler Moss, Andrei Trefilov and Tyrone Garner also saw playing time, but no one was able to step up and become the team's number one goaltender. Their goals-against averages ranged from Brathwaite's 2.45 to Garner's 5.18.

The team's record showed a slight improvement from the season before with 30 wins, 40 losses and 12 ties. But it still wasn't good enough for a playoff spot. That made for three years without post-season play, and the fans in Calgary were starting to tune out. Between the 1987–88 and the 1995–96 seasons, an average of 19,000 fans had shown up to watch the Flames play. As the team's fortunes began to slip, so did fan numbers. By the time the 1999–2000 season got underway, barely 15,000 fans were bothering to show up. The Saddledome resembled a perpetual Christmas decoration with empty green seats visible beside swaths of fans dressed in red Flames jerseys. The stadium even had a new name: oil and gas company Pengrowth forked out for the naming rights and christened it the "Pengrowth Saddledome."

Valeri Bure scored 35 goals that season. Jarome Iginla flirted with the 30-goal mark but didn't make good, finishing the year with only 29. Center Marc Savard scored 22. The next-highest goal total on the team was forward Jeff Shantz's 13. Only 12 players on the roster played more than 50 games during the year. One of those players was Robyn Regehr, the defense-man acquired from Colorado in the Theoren Fleury trade. He showed plenty of promise, scoring 5 goals and 7 assists in 57 games on the Flames' blue line.

Fred Brathwaite won the starting job between the pipes for the Flames and was joined by a surprising face, another ex-Edmonton Oiler legend named Grant Fuhr. The pair managed to win 30 games in the 1999–2000 season.

The team's record of 31 wins, 36 losses, 10 ties and 5 overtime losses wasn't good enough to make the playoffs. It wasn't good enough to save the Flames' coach's job either. In 2000, both Coates and Sutter were removed from their positions with the team. Former Flames' assistant Don Hay, who had exactly one season of head coaching experience in Phoenix under his belt, was given the coaching job in Calgary. Craig Button, the former director of player personnel for the Dallas Stars, became the Flames' new general manager.

Hay's coaching career with the Flames would last less than one season as the Calgary Flames regressed in 2000–01. Before the season even ended, with the Flames already assured of missing the post-season with a record of 27 wins, 36 losses, 15 ties and 4 overtime losses, Hay was pushed aside in favor of Greg Gilbert. A former Chicago Blackhawks player turned coach, Gilbert inherited a team that was starting to show flashes of talent but couldn't seem to string together more than one win at a time.

In the 2000–01 season, Iginla scored 31 times, finally passing the 30-goal mark. Savard, Bure and Cory Stillman each scored more than 20 goals. The team had acquired Dave Lowry, a veteran center from the San Jose Sharks who scored 18 goals and 17 assists in 79 games, a career best. Craig Conroy joined the Flames near the end of the season, scoring seven points in 14 games. No one else scored more than 10 goals.

At the end of the 1999–2000 season, Grant Fuhr retired. Rather than promote one of their young goalies to fill his spot as Fred Brathwaite's backup, the Flames instead reached into their past and brought back Mike Vernon. Since leaving the Flames in 1995, the pint-sized puckstopper had won a Stanley Cup with the Detroit Red Wings and played in San Jose with the Sharks and in Florida with the Panthers. In 41 games in the 2000–01 season, Vernon won only 12 and posted a goals-against average of 3.23. But then, Brathwaite hadn't done much better, winning only 15 of 49 starts.

In the summer of 2001–02, Button went shopping for a goaltender. The team needed a well-known puckstopper they could count on to make big saves when they needed them. Button decided on St. Louis' Roman Turek, who had fallen out of favor in Missouri after a poor playoff performance the year before. In exchange for Turek, Calgary traded Brathwaite and forwards Daniel Tkaczuk and Sergei Varlamov.

Button also went shopping for more offense, sending Valeri Bure, who was not proving to be a team player, and Jason Wiemer to Florida in exchange for Rob Neidermayer.

When the Flames took to the ice for the 2001–02 season, the team was vastly improved from the one that had played the last six years. The fans seemed to take a renewed interest in the team as well. In one memorable incident during a home game on October 17, a drunken fan named Tim Hurlbut leapt over the glass onto the ice during a stoppage in play clad in nothing but a pair of red socks. Unfortunately, the alcohol interfered with Hurlbut's dexterity, and he slipped as he came over the glass, falling awkwardly and cracking his head on the ice. After lying there for six minutes, exposed to the entire world, paramedics carted him off.

Despite their improved lineup and burst of fan enthusiasm, the Flames couldn't improve the one thing that counted most—the notches under their win column.

But they did come close to making the playoffs in 2001–02, largely because of the efforts of two players: Roman Turek and Jarome Iginla. The team finished with its best record in four years with 32 win, 35 losses, 12 ties and 3 overtime losses. In his first season wearing the flaming "C," Turek played a whopping 69 games, winning 30 and posting a 2.53 goals-against average. It was Turek's absence from the ice that cost the team a playoff spot because Mike Vernon won only two of his 18 starts.

Jarome Iginla, who improved steadily season after season, caught fire in 2001–02. He became the first Calgary Flame since Theoren Fleury to score more than 50 goals, finishing the year with 52 goals and 44 assists. Iginla was part of a dynamic trio up front that included center

Craig Conroy and winger Dean McAmmond. The three linemates finished on top of the scoring ranks with Conroy's 26 goals earning him second and McAmmond's 21 earning him third.

Iginla's play earned him a raft of hardware at the NHL's annual awards gala at the end of the playoffs, including the Rocket Richard Trophy for most goals and the Art Ross Trophy for most points. The players also voted to give him the Lester B. Pearson award for the league's most valuable player. It was the perfect cap to a great season.

The Flames' forward also played for Team Canada at the Winter Olympics in Salt Lake City and was a key member of the gold medal–winning team.

After the improvements in 2001–02, everyone expected the Flames to make the playoffs in the 2002–03 season. But everyone was wrong. The Flames stumbled out of the gate, winning only three of their first 10 games, and by December, the Flames had again set up shop near the bottom of the league rankings. Calgary fans were running out of patience, and the ownership group wanted to start seeing some post-season revenue. The team fired Greg Gilbert on December 3, 2002, and quickly appointed Al MacNeil as the interim coach.

MacNeil had been the team's head coach during its days in Atlanta. After being pushed out of that post, he continued to work with the team in upper management, following them when they moved to Calgary.

After shopping around for two weeks, the team finally found the permanent coach they were looking for in Darryl Sutter. Sutter was one of five brothers from Viking, Alberta, who had become an integral part of the NHL game. He had played eight years for the Chicago Blackhawks and had coached the team in the mid-90s. More importantly, he had just been fired as coach of the San Jose Sharks at the beginning of December. Now Button wanted him to come in and turn the Flames into a winning squad.

Sutter believed he was the right man for the job but knew it would take time. However talented he was, he wouldn't be able to turn the Flames around overnight.

The team finished the year with a record of 29 wins, 36 losses, 13 ties and 4 overtime losses, again missing the playoffs. Iginla posted only 35 goals and 67 points. Conroy scored 22. The third member of the previous year's lineup, Dean McAmmond, had been traded to Colorado at the beginning of the season along with Derek Morris in exchange for talented American winger Chris Drury. At the trade deadline, Calgary traded a draft pick to bring McAmmond back. Unfortunately for the Flames, no one on either team knew of an obscure rule that did not allow a team to trade a player away and reacquire him in the same season. The trade was allowed to stand, but McAmmond was not allowed to play in the team's 12 remaining games.

Drury played well for the Flames, scoring 23 goals and 30 assists. The team also added NHL journeyman forward Martin Gelinas and center Stephane Yelle. Roman Turek slipped in his second season with the team, winning only 27 of 65 starts. With Vernon retiring at the end of the previous season, perennial backup goalie Jamie McLennan took over, but he was able to win only two of his 22 starts.

Darryl Sutter believed he had a team with unlimited potential. But there was something missing. Whatever it was, Sutter would be responsible for finding it. During the off-season, he replaced Button as general manager of the Calgary Flames.

Chapter Ten

A Magical Run

When the 2003–04 season opened in October, many Flames fans figured Calgary was due for a successful season. True, the team had not seen a whiff of playoff action since 1996, but they had been flirting with success for the last two seasons. Roman Turek's and Jarome Iginla's stellar play were an integral part of those successes. Now the Flames needed to master the art of winning consistently.

Darryl Sutter was still the coach but was now the general manager as well, which meant he was responsible not only for the quality of the team's game on the ice, but also for making sure the team had the tools they needed to win.

The Flames started off the 2003–04 season with a 4–1 away-game loss to the Vancouver Canucks. Sutter's squad rebounded to win its next two games on home ice by scores of 3–2 and 1–0. But they quickly returned to their losing ways.

By mid-November, the Flames were obviously slipping as they had won only six games while losing 10, were 14th in the Western Conference and were six spots away from a playoff spot.

During the team's second game of the season, the Flames beat San Jose 3–2. But they sustained what looked like a crippling blow to their chances of making the playoffs. During the second period, the Sharks' Alyn McCauley broke in alone on Turek during a bad Calgary line change, deked the Flames' goaltender to the ice and scored. McCauly collided with Turek, as the puck slipped into the net, inadvertently kneeing the Flames' starting goaltender in the head. Turek had to be helped off the ice, and Jamie McLennan quickly took over between the pipes.

Turek returned to the lineup a week later, but lasted less than three days when he injured his knee during a game. McLennan again took over in goal, doing his best to keep the Flames competitive. But McLennan was simply a backup goalie and couldn't be asked to carry the entire team on his shoulders. With Turek's knee showing no signs of healing quickly, Darryl Sutter went out looking for another goaltender. He set his sights on an older Finnish netminder he knew from his days as coach of the San Jose Sharks, Miikka Kiprusoff. Kiprusoff was now playing as the Sharks' third-string goaltender.

On November 16, Sutter picked up the puckstopper in exchange for a second-round draft pick.

Although he hadn't played much with San
Jose that season, Kiprusoff was thrust into the
limelight as Calgary's number-one goalie. He
rose to the challenge nicely. Two days after the
trade, "Kipper" stepped in between the pipes at
the Saddledome in a faceoff against the Montréal
Canadiens. He proceeded to turn away 22 of 23
Montréal shots in a 2–1 Flames win. One night
later, Chicago came to town, and Kiprusoff again
slammed closed the net, stopping 24 of 25 shots
in another 2–1 victory.

Over the next 16 games, Calgary turned in
one of its most impressive runs to date, winning
13 and losing only three. The streak pushed them
out of the basement in the West and into a competitive position in the league.

Unfortunately, the Flames were hounded by
injuries. On December 31, in a game against the
Colorado Avalanche, Kiprusoff sprained his knee
and left the game. The injury sidelined him for
the next six weeks and McLennan again found
himself thrust into the role of starting goaltender. Without Kiprusoff, the Flames started to
lose, winning only four of their next 13 games.
Roman Turek finally returned to the lineup in
January, but couldn't seem to match the standard of play Kiprusoff had set. When Kipper

returned in late February, he immediately supplanted Turek as the starter, and the Flames started winning again.

Their new goaltender wasn't the only reason for the Flames' success. Jarome Iginla was having another standout year for Calgary. Martin Gelinas was playing great two-way hockey and was scoring clutch goals for the team. The defensive unit, anchored by Jordan Leopold, Robyn Regehr, Rhett Warrener and Denis Gauthier, was doing a good job of clearing away the front of the net so Kiprusoff could see the action in front of him.

The Flames were also pulling together as a team—no one player was considered better than anyone else. Craig Conroy, who had played in St. Louis before coming to the Flames, introduced a tradition from his old team, awarding a green construction worker's hardhat to the unsung hero of every game. The team also started having a little fun both on and off the ice. Starting in January, journalists and play-by-play announcers noticed that most of the players were sporting hair on their upper lips. It turned out the team had decided to hold a "mustache-growing contest." Some players, like Dave Lowry, did quite well. Others, like Jarome Iginla, did not.

By March, the Flames weren't just fighting for a playoff spot; they were battling with Vancouver for home-ice advantage. In the end, the Canucks finished first in the Northwest Division. Colorado came in second. The Flames secured the third spot in the division and the sixth in the conference with their first winning record in years with 42 wins, 30 losses, 7 ties and 3 overtime losses.

Iginla continued to lead the team in both goals and scoring, finishing the year with 41 goals and 32 assists. A significant number of those goals came off passes from Craig Conroy, who scored only eight goals but added a team-high 39 assists. Shean Donovan scored 18 goals. Gelinas and McAmmond each scored 17.

Although Calgary wasn't going to set any goal-scoring records, with a goaltender like Kiprusoff, they didn't need to. The Kipper was the story of the season, winning 24 of 38 starts, losing only 10 and tying four. His 1.69 goals-against average stood as the lowest recorded by a goaltender in modern hockey history. But, as the Flames had proven throughout their team's history, the regular season was one thing, the playoffs another. As the team traveled to Vancouver to take on the Canucks in the first round, everyone wondered just how long the Flames would last—or how fast they would lose—in this post-season.

Game one opened up on April 7 in Vancouver. Sutter would confess after the game that his team appeared nervous and consequently didn't play as well as they could have. Vancouver scored four power-play goals and popped in a fifth on a delayed penalty call to take the first game by 5–3. Oleg Saprykin, Chris Simon and Kryzstof Oliwa each scored for the Flames.

"I thought our top players had a jittery night," said Sutter. "And even at that, we almost won."

With their playoff nerves effectively exorcised, Calgary came back to the ice at General Motors Place and immediately took the game to Vancouver. Jarome Iginla scored early in the first period, walking out from behind the net and burying a wrist shot past Dan Cloutier. Matthew Lombardi scored 50 seconds later to give the Flames a 2–0 lead. Kiprusoff turned aside 25 shots, surrendering only one goal to Canucks captain Markus Naslund.

"Last game it was all power-play goals. Today we killed better and that was the difference," said Kiprusoff.

The series shifted back to Calgary, where both teams played a solid defensive battle in game three. Unfortunately for Calgary, the Canucks came up with one more goal than the Flames in a 2–1 win. There was one silver lining to the Flames' loss—Canucks goalie Dan Cloutier left the game with an injured knee and didn't return, forcing backup Johan Hedberg between the pipes.

Approximately 18,300 fans packed the Saddledome for game four, and they were rewarded with a 4–0 Flames victory on home ice. Kiprusoff turned aside 20 shots for the goose egg while Stephane Yelle, Chris Clark, Donovan and Iginla each put goals on the board.

The teams returned to Vancouver tied at two wins each. The Flames clearly had the momentum in the series, and Canucks coach Mike Crawford tried to disrupt that by switching goalies, giving rookie Alex Auld his first-ever playoff start. But the Flames couldn't be stopped. They took game five by a score of 2–1, with Iginla scoring the winner and assisting on Craig Conroy's goal. Heading back to Calgary, the Flames were sure they had the series wrapped up.

But Calgary stumbled out of the opening faceoff in game six, as if they weren't sure what they needed to do to win. Needing a victory to avoid elimination, the Canucks had put four goals past Kiprusoff by the second period, taking a 4–0 lead. Rather than give up, the Flames' Ville Nieminen, Martin Gelinas, Saprykin and Clark each scored, forcing the game into overtime. Just over two minutes into the third overtime period, the Canucks' Brendan Morrison buried the puck past Kiprusoff to force a seventh game.

Jarome Iginla opened game seven with his fourth goal of the series, but the Canucks tied the game in the third. Iginla scored again to put Calgary up by one, but Vancouver stormed back and tied the game on a Matt Cooke goal. No one else scored, and the game went to overtime.

This game didn't take as long as the previous one had. Barely one minute into overtime, Iginla fired a shot on net that Auld turned aside. The rebound went straight to Gelinas who buried it. The Flames had won the game and the series.

"In my 25 years of hockey, that was the single most dominant game I've ever seen a player play," Sutter said of Iginla afterwards. The forward had chipped in on all three Calgary goals.

Calgary's next playoff date would come in Detroit against the Red Wings, who had finished first in the league in the regular season. If Calgary was supposed to be intimidated by the Red Wings, they didn't show it in game one. Tied 1–1 at the end of regulation, Marcus Nilson scored the game-winning goal off a Martin Gelinas pass 2 minutes and 39 seconds into overtime to give the Flames a 1–0 series lead.

"It's a huge win," said Kiprusoff. "But that game's behind us, and we have to be ready to play the next game."

Detroit proved to be more ready than the Flames in their next match-up. They fired 32 shots on Kiprusoff, putting four of them in the net. The Red Wings won the game 5–2, splitting the series 1–1 as the faceoff moved to Calgary. In game three, Shean Donovan broke a 2–2 tie half-way through the third period to give the Flames a 3–2 win. The Red Wings took control of game four early, scoring 26 seconds in and adding a second goal two minutes later. Calgary tied the game when Nieminen and Gelinas scored two goals in 18 seconds. Mathieu Dandenault scored the game winner, and Henrik Zetterberg added an empty-netter to seal the Flames' victory.

As good as the Red Wings tried to be in game five, Miikka Kiprusoff was better. The Finnish Flame turned aside 31 shots, and Craig Conroy's second-period goal gave Calgary a 1–0 lead. Detroit captain Steve Yzerman took a puck to the eye and was forced to leave the game. He did not return for the rest of the series, sidelined by fractures in both his eye and cheekbones. Yzerman was the heart of the Detroit Red Wings, and his teammates could do little without him.

Game six in Calgary went down to the wire. Both Red Wings goaltender Curtis Joseph and Kiprusoff played their hearts out, turning aside every single shot in regulation time. With less than a minute left to play in the first overtime period, Jarome Iginla fired a shot on net out of the right corner. The rebound went to Craig Conroy who launched one toward the net. But his shot caromed off a skate on the way to the net and bounced right to Martin Gelinas who couldn't have missed the yawning cage if he had tried. The goal was Gelinas' second series-clinching goal, giving the Flames a 4–2 series win over the heavily favored Red Wings. Gelinas' performance in the clutch earned him the nickname "The Eliminator."

"Our team's been resilient," Gelinas said. "I was in the right place at the right time, and the rebound came right to me."

More impressive were Kiprusoff's back-to-back shutouts of Detroit. In 149 minutes and 11 seconds of play, Kiprusoff had not surrendered a single goal.

"To shut out the Wings back-to-back, he's been awesome," said Iginla.

Next up were the San Jose Sharks. The two teams would be playing for the Conference Championship, and the winner would go on to play in the Stanley Cup final. The Flames staked out their claim in game one as Kiprusoff turned aside 49 shots from his old team during regulation and overtime play. The Flames' Steve Montador provided the overtime winner, giving the team a 4–3 win and 1–0 series lead. Calgary carried their momentum to San Jose for game two, putting four goals past the Sharks' goaltender Evgeni Nabokov. Kiprusoff surrendered only one. Heading back to Calgary, the Flames were now up two games in the series.

Once again the Flames played poorly in front of their home crowd. The Sharks, led by Nabokov, held Calgary scoreless but posted three goals of their own to win game three 3–0. While the Flames scored twice on Nabokov in game four, the Sharks managed to score four of their own. San Jose had won their second-straight game 4–2. Darryl Sutter blamed the loss on his team's mental approach to the game.

"Turnovers cost us the game; no doubt about it," he said.

Since the playoffs had begun, the Flames always seemed to play their best hockey on the road. The pattern held when the team rolled into San Jose on May 17 for game five. When they rolled out of town they had a 3–0 victory under their belt and a 3–2 series lead. Iginla, Nieminen and Conroy all scored in the win. Kiprusoff stopped 19 shots for his fourth playoff shutout. Intent on preserving their road magic, Sutter ordered all of his players to spend the night before game six at a hotel in downtown Calgary. He wanted to give them that "road feeling." Crazy as it sounded, the strategy seemed to work. Martin Gelinas proved once again that he was "The Eliminator": for the third time this playoff year, he scored the series-winning goal in the second period. The Flames won game six 3–1, taking the series 4–2.

For the first time in 15 years and for only the third time in franchise history, the team was headed for the Stanley Cup finals. They were the first Canadian team to play for the Stanley Cup since 1994. The players knew how special this moment was.

"You never know when this opportunity is going to come again in your life," said Iginla.

In the finals, the Flames squared off against the Tampa Bay Lightning. It was the first time in their history that the Flames' opponents in the final series would not be the Montréal Canadiens. The Lightning was led by former Flame Martin St. Louis, dazzling forward Vincent Lecavalier and goaltender Nikolai Khabibulin. They had taken out the New York Islanders in the first round, the Canadiens in the second round and the Philadelphia Flyers in the third. Tampa had finished first in the Eastern Conference during the regular season—the Flames had finished sixth—which guaranteed them home ice advantage in the final.

Back home in Calgary, the Flames' fans were celebrating their team's success. Flames jerseys were selling out everywhere. Soon it was impossible to find one anywhere in the entire city. After every game, home or away, tens of thousands of fans poured onto the city's 17th Avenue South West to celebrate. The stretch became known as the "Red Mile." Even die-hard Oilers fans in Edmonton were rooting for the hated Flames.

Three million viewers tuned in to watch game one of the Stanley Cup final on CBC's *Hockey Night in Canada*, the show's second biggest audience in history. The Flames' Andrew Ferrence opened the scoring in the first period to give Calgary a 1–0 lead. Iginla doubled the lead on a breakaway later in the period when he corralled his own rebound and buried it. Three minutes after that, Stephane Yelle scored a high wrist shot to put Calgary up 3–0. The Lightning's Martin St. Louis eventually scored for Tampa Bay, but Calgary added an empty-netter to win 4–1.

As heroic as he'd been to date in the playoffs, Miikka Kiprusoff looked all too human in game two. Tampa Bay buried four goals in his net before Calgary even got on the scoreboard. The Lightning took the game 4–1.

The series returned to Calgary tied at one game apiece. In game three, Kiprusoff shook off his poor performance and stopped every single shot the Lightning sent his way. Simon, Donovan and Iginla all scored to give Calgary a 3–0 win. Iginla finished the game with a "Gordie Howe hat trick," scoring a goal and assisting on Simon's goal before dropping his gloves to fight the Lightning's Vincent Lecavalier.

Game four did not start well for the Flames. At the 1:52 mark of the first period, referee Kerry Fraser called Chris Clark for cross-checking at the same time the second referee, Brad Watson, called Mike Commodore for holding. The result was a 5-on-3 power play on which Brad Richards successfully converted. The Lightning would hold off the Flames' offense for the rest of the game, winning 1–0 and evening out the series at two games apiece.

In game five, the series headed back to Tampa Bay for one of the most thrilling playoff games in recent memory. It had everything: great goaltending, plenty of scoring chances and overtime. Gelinas opened the scoring during the power play barely two minutes into the first period. Then St. Louis scored for Tampa Bay, tying the game at one all. In the second period, Iginla came flying down the wing and wired a slapshot past the Lightning's goaltender, Khabibulin, to put the Flames up 2–1. Soon after, the Lightning again tied the game on a Fredrik Modin power-play goal. It took just under 15 minutes of overtime to decide the game, but it was decided in the Flames' favor when Saprykin picked up Iginla's rebound and buried it behind Khabibulin to give the Flames a chokehold on the series.

The night of game six, the Stanley Cup arrived at Pengrowth Saddledome and was made ready to be presented if the Flames won. The Lightning's Brad Richards opened the scoring on a power play, but the Flames' Chris Clark responded by slamming home a backdoor pass to tie the game. Richards scored again less than a minute later to give Tampa Bay a 2–1 lead, but the Flames' Marcus Nilson again tied the game halfway through the second period.

With just under seven minutes left to go in regulation time, Saprykin slipped a pass to Martin Gelinas, who was dashing in on goal. But the puck caromed off of Gelinas' skate and slipped underneath Khabibulin, who got his right leg on the puck. No one blew the whistle, and no one on the Flames' team bothered arguing. They didn't know that video replay showed the puck might have crossed the goal line. Had the goal counted, it would have been Gelinas' fourth straight series-winning goal. But it didn't, and the game went into overtime.

One overtime period went by without determining a winner. Then 27 seconds into the second overtime, Martin St. Louis scored the game winner. The goal forced the series into a dramatic game seven. It was the stuff of boyhood dreams, the Stanley Cup riding on one win in one game. And the Flames would play for the Cup on the road.

Ruslan Fedotenko opened the scoring for the Lightning, banging in a Brad Richards rebound during a power play to take a 1–0 lead. Fedotenko scored again in the second period, taking a beautiful pass from Lecavalier and banging it high over Kiprusoff's glove. Calgary pulled to within one goal in the third when Craig Conroy fired a bullet from the point that eluded Khabibulin. With time winding down, Sutter called Kiprusoff to the bench for the extra attacker. It was no use. The clock ran down to zero, and Tampa Bay ran off with the Stanley Cup.

"We thought that was going to be us out there, hearing that music, listening to the crowd, lifting that Cup," a teary-eyed Iginla said later. "We wanted to win it for Calgary, our city, the fans who've been so great to us—the best in the league. They showed what a sports city is. We worked...so hard. We got so close."

The team did, however, walk away with some hardware even if it wasn't the Stanley Cup. Iginla shared the Rocket Richard Trophy for most goals with Atlanta Thrasher's forward Ilya Kovalchuk and Columbus Blue Jackets marvel Rick Nash.

Despite the loss, the Flames' fans hoped that a team that did this well in the playoffs could perform just as well the next season. Unfortunately, they had to wait awhile to find out if their hope was justified because the next NHL season was a long time in coming.

Chapter Eleven

Post-Lockout Hockey

Any chance the Flames had of following up their Stanley Cup run in the 2004–05 season was cut short before it even started.

The collective bargaining agreement between the league and the National Hockey League Players Association (NHLPA) had expired, and there was little reason to expect a new agreement would be negotiated before the season began. The owners wanted to reduce out-of-control player salaries and link salaries to revenues. The disagreement escalated into a standoff. The owners were not going to cave to the players just for the sake of playing hockey, and the players weren't about to give up their ability to market themselves to the highest bidder. On September 29, 2004, Gary Bettman announced the regular season would not begin until the owners could guarantee "cost certainty," which meant imposing a cap on team salaries.

In negotiations, the players offered a 24 percent salary rollback, but the league refused it because the offer didn't cap salaries. As the winter stretched on with no hockey, 350 players spent the season playing for club teams in Europe. Other players started dissenting from the NHLPA's position saying they would accept a salary cap. Of the owners involved in the negotiations, Flames governor Harley Hotchkiss became one of their key horse traders and spokesmen. Even after the league cancelled the season outright in February, Hotchkiss continued working towards making sure there would be hockey the following year.

The stalemate ended in July 2005 when both the league and the union ratified a new agreement that capped salaries and linked them to revenue. In order to attract fans who had been turned off by the lockout, the league also amended many of its rules. They reintroduced tag-up offsides as well as two-line offsides. They also penalized goaltenders for handling the puck outside a specific zone behind the net to open up the game, to allow it to flow freely and to keep it exciting. Finally, they introduced the shoot-out, a staple of international hockey, to settle games tied at the end of regulation time to create more excitement. The league also reaffirmed its commitment to cracking down on the hooking, holding and overall obstructive play that prevented the NHL's best players from showcasing their speed and talent.

In Calgary, the Flames settled some potentially troublesome business matters before the season even started. In August 2004, they signed Iginla to a new three-year, $21 million contract. The team picked up Tony Amonte, a former 40-goal scorer with the Chicago Blackhawks, to a two-year deal and added bruising right-winger Darren McCarty to their lineup. They re-signed Miikka Kiprusoff to a three-year, $10 million contract and brought in former Oilers standout defenseman Roma Hamrlik. Unfortunately, Craig Conroy and Martin Gelinas left the team.

The biggest addition for the 2005–06 season was to the defense. After a stellar junior career, the Flames signed 2003 first-round draft choice Dion Phaneuf. The Edmonton, Alberta native had been banging bodies for the Red Deer Rebels since 2001 and was finally ready to play in the NHL. Phaneuf could hit hard, had a cannon of a shot off the point and could quarterback power plays. In short, he was the big defenseman the Flames had been looking for.

Many sports writers, including those at magazines such as *Sports Illustrated*, picked the Flames to finish first overall in the league in the 2005–06 season and to win the Stanley Cup. The Flames did play a great season, but their regular season finish was not as strong as they had predicted. At 46 wins, 25 losses and 11 shootout or overtime losses, their record wasn't the best in the league, but at 103 points, they were first overall in the division and third in the conference.

Iginla led the Flames in scoring again with 35 goals and 32 assists. Damon Langkow backed him up with 25 goals and 24 assists of his own. Phaneuf disappointed no one in his first year, scoring 20 goals from the blue line and adding 29 assists. In fact, Phaneuf could easily have run away with the Calder Trophy if his debut in the NHL hadn't coincided with those of Sidney Crosby and Alexander Ovechkin. Kiprusoff proved he was worth the money the Flames were paying him, winning 42 of 74 starts and posting a goals-against average of 2.07.

The Flames' third-place finish meant they would take on the Anaheim Mighty Ducks in the first round of the playoffs. The Ducks' lineup featured former Flames prospect Jean-Sebastien Giguère, who had made a name for himself in the Anaheim's surprising playoff run of 2003. Giguère, however, had been supplanted during the regular season by Russian goaltender Ilya Bryzgalov in net, who proved to be one of the deciding factors of the series.

Almost everyone picked the Flames to win the series, but the Ducks weren't listening. Led by Teemu Selanne, Joffrey Lupul and the stellar goaltending of Bryzgalov, the Ducks shocked the hockey world by upsetting the Calgary in seven games, sending the Flames packing.

"Disappointing doesn't even begin to describe the feeling," Robyn Regehr said. "All the hard work these guys put in through the regular season to get home-ice advantage. And we do not come out and take advantage of that."

During the off-season, the Flames made two big moves. The first came behind the bench as Darryl Sutter announced he was stepping down as coach, but staying on as general manager. Sutter appointed Jim Playfair, an assistant with the team for the last three seasons, as the Flames' new head coach.

Sutter also went looking for more offense on the ice. He wanted another forward who could take some of the burden off of Jarome Iginla. On June 24, 2006, Sutter traded defenseman Jordan Leopold, a second-round pick in the 2006 draft and a conditional draft pick to the Colorado Avalanche, for winger Alex Tanguay. In his seven-year career with the Avalanche, the winger had hit the 20-goal mark three times.

Again the Flames went in to training camp touted by many as the likely first-place team and the likely Stanley Cup champion. After spending so long without anyone counting on them for anything, it is new for the Flames to be touted as the best of the best. But, then, Calgary has always been a team full of surprises.

The Stats

Legend	
GP – Games Played	OT – Overtime
W – Wins	GF – Goals For
L – Loses	GA – Goals Against
T – Ties	PIM – Penalty in Minutes

Scoring Leaders

Players	Games Played	Goals	Assists	Points
Theoren Fleury	791	364	466	830
Al MacInnis	803	213	609	822
Joe Nieuwendyk	577	314	302	616
Jarome Iginla	726	294	297	591
Gary Suter	617	128	437	565
Kent Nilsson	425	229	333	562
Guy Chouinard	514	193	336	529
Gary Roberts	585	257	248	505
Eric Vail	539	206	246	452
Paul Reinhart	517	109	336	445

Season-by-Season Record in the National Hockey League

Season	W	L	T	OT	GF	GA	Points
1972–73	25	38	15	N/A	191	239	65
1973–74	30	34	14	N/A	214	239	74
1974–75	34	31	15	N/A	243	233	83
1975–76	35	33	12	N/A	262	237	82
1976–77	34	34	12	N/A	264	265	80
1977–78	34	27	19	N/A	274	252	87
1978–79	41	31	8	N/A	327	280	90
1979–80	35	32	13	N/A	282	269	83
1980–81	39	27	14	N/A	329	298	92
1981–82	29	34	17	N/A	334	345	75
1982–83	32	34	14	N/A	321	317	78
1983–84	34	32	14	N/A	311	314	82
1984–85	41	27	12	N/A	363	302	94
1985–86	40	31	9	N/A	354	315	89
1986–87	46	31	3	N/A	318	289	95
1987–88	48	23	9	N/A	397	305	105
1988–89	54	17	9	N/A	354	226	117
1989–90	42	23	15	N/A	348	265	99
1990–91	46	26	8	N/A	344	263	100
1991–92	31	37	12	N/A	296	305	74
1992–93	43	30	11	N/A	322	282	97
1993–94	42	29	13	N/A	302	256	97
1994–95	24	17	7	N/A	163	135	55
1995–96	34	37	11	N/A	241	240	79
1996–97	32	41	9	N/A	214	239	73
1997–98	26	41	15	N/A	217	252	67
1998–99	30	40	12	N/A	211	234	72
1999–2000	31	36	10	5	211	256	77
2000–01	27	36	15	4	197	236	73
2001–02	32	35	15	3	201	220	79
2002–03	29	36	13	4	186	228	75
2003–04	42	30	7	3	200	176	94
2004–05	Season cancelled due to lockout						
2005–06	46	25	N/A	11	218	200	103

Season and Playoff Record

Season	Regular Season Finish	Playoffs
1972–73	Seventh, West	Missed Playoffs
1973–74	Fourth, West	Lost Quarterfinal
1974–75	Fourth, Patrick Division	Missed Playoffs
1975–76	Third, Patrick Division	Lost Preliminary Round
1976–77	Third, Patrick Division	Lost Preliminary Round
1977–78	Third, Patrick Division	Lost Preliminary Round
1978–79	Fourth, Patrick Division	Lost Preliminary Round
1979–80	Fourth, Patrick Division	Lost Preliminary Round
1980–81	Fifth, Patrick Division	Lost Stanley Cup Semifinal
1981–82	Fifth, Smythe Division	Lost Division Semifinal
1982–83	Second, Smythe Division	Lost Smythe Division Final
1983–84	Second, Smythe Division	Lost Smythe Division Final
1984–85	Third, Smythe Division	Lost Smythe Division Semifinal
1985–86	Second, Smythe Division	Lost Stanley Cup Final
1986–87	Second, Smythe Division	Lost Smythe Division Semifinal
1987–88	First, Smythe Division	Lost Smythe Division Final
1988–89	First, Smythe Division	Won Stanley Cup
1989–90	First, Smythe Division	Lost Division Semifinal
1990–91	Second, Smythe Division	Lost Division Semifinal
1991–92	Fifth, Smythe Division	Missed Playoffs
1992–93	Second, Smythe Division	Lost Division Semifinal
1993–94	First, Pacific Division	Lost Conference Quarterfinal
1994–95	First, Pacific Division	Lost Conference Quarterfinal
1995–96	Second, Pacific Division	Lost Conference Quarterfinal
1996–97	Fifth, Pacific Division	Missed Playoffs
1997–98	Fifth, Pacific Division	Missed Playoffs
1998–99	Third, Pacific Division	Missed Playoffs
1999–2000	Fourth, Northwest	Missed Playoffs
2000–01	Fourth, Northwest	Missed Playoffs
2001–02	Fourth, Northwest	Missed Playoffs
2002–03	Fifth, Northwest	Missed Playoffs
2003–04	Third, Northwest	Lost Stanley Cup Final
2004–05	Season cancelled due to lockout	
2005–06	First, Northwest	Lost Conference Quarterfinal

Notes on Sources

Boer, Peter. *Weird Facts About Canadian Hockey*. Montréal: OverTime Books, 2005.

Boer, Peter. *The Edmonton Oilers*. Montréal: OverTime Books, 2006.

Hanson, George and Short, John. *Fire On Ice: The Flames*. Los Angeles: Executive Sports Publications, 1982.

Johnson, George et al. *Calgary Flames: The Fire Inside*. Toronto: CanWest Books, 2006.

Jones, Terry. *Calgary Flames*. Mankato: Creative Education, 1996.

Podnieks, Andrew. *The Flames: Celebrating Calgary's Dream Season, 2003–04*. Bolton: Fenn Publishing Company, 2004.

Rennie, Ross. *Calgary Flames*. Mankato: Creative Education, 1990.

Web Sources

C of Red (n.d.). www.calgaryflames.com.
Retrieved September 3 to November 26, 2006.

The Internet Hockey Database (n.d.). www.hockeydb.com.
Retrieved September 2 to November 26, 2006.

The National Hockey League Website (n.d.). www.nhl.com.
Retrieved October 13 to November 26, 2006.

Sportsnet.ca (n.d.). www.sportsnet.ca.
Retrieved September 4 to November 26, 2006.

The Goaltender Home Page (n.d.). www.hockeygoalies.org.
Retrieved October 5 to November 26, 2006.

Hockey Draft Central (n.d.). www.hockeydraftcentral.com.
Retrieved September 17 to November 23, 2006.

databaseHockey.com (n.d.). www.databasehockey.com.
Retrieved September 8 to November 26, 2006.

Wikipedia, the free encyclopedia (n.d.). en.wikipedia.org.
Retrieved October 18 to November 26, 2006.

CBC Sports Online: NHL Playoffs 2006 (May, 2006).
www.cbc.ca/sports/hockey/stanleycup2006/storyview.
html?/story/stanleycup2006/national/2006/05/03/
Sports/mightyducks-flames060503.html.
Retrieved November 24, 2006.

Peter Boer

Peter Boer has been a consummate hockey fan since his parents first bribed him with a chocolate bar to skate from the red line to the blue line at the age of four. It took him three years to score his first goal, but he never looked back. Since realizing actual talent was a necessary requirement for an NHL career, Peter has immersed himself in the game in other ways. He has refereed and minded the score clock for beer-league hockey, coached women's hockey and been a goal judge, penalty box staff, security guard, ticket taker and blood cleaner for the CIS University of Alberta Golden Bears and Concordia University Stingers.

When he's not spending his Saturday nights bemoaning the current state of the NHL, Peter is the assistant editor for the *St. Albert Gazette*. He is the author of five other non-fiction books, including *Weird Facts About Canadian Hockey* and *The Edmonton Oilers*. This is his third OverTime book.